Best Wishes

to

Freneed

CRUSADERS FOR JUSTICE

A CHRONICLE OF PROTEST BY AGITATORS,
ADVOCATES AND ACTIVISTS IN THEIR STRUGGLE
FOR CIVIL AND HUMAN RIGHTS IN ST. PAUL,
MINNESOTA, 1802–1985.

Jason

ARTHUR C. MCWATT

Arthur C McWatt

St. Paul Branch of the NAACP
St. Paul, Minnesota

McWatt, Arthur C.
Crusaders for Justice: A Chronicle of Protest by Agitators, Advocates and Activists in their Struggle for Civil and Human Rights in St. Paul, Minnesota 1802–1985

Photo credits pp. 235 - 236

The St. Paul NAACP produced this publication for educational and non-profit purposes.

ISBN-10: 0-9675581-8-2
ISBN-13: 978-0-9675581-8-9

With Assistance from

Papyrus Publishing Inc.
Brooklyn Park, Minnesota, United States of America
55428

PapyrusPublishing@msn.com

DEDICATED
TO

"Those courageous and devoted advocates who repeatedly pursued constitutional rights and human equalities for those who had been denied them; persistently contesting the personal privileges of the majority and enlightening the African-American community to the nature of white supremacy and its possible consequences both to those oppressed and its oppressors."

Foreword

Since about the mid-1970s there has been a growing stock of publications regarding the African American experience in the state of Minnesota; pamphlets, booklets, books and other salient works have been written in several genres. Among the most notable have been memoirs and biographies by the late former St. Paul Police Deputy Chief James Griffin, the late Evelyn Fairbanks, the late Nellie Stone Johnson and the late W. Harry Davis. Griffin and Fairbanks have left us beautifully arresting images of "The Rondo Community" in St. Paul. Likewise, Davis has given reflections capturing family and community in Near North Minneapolis, and Stone Johnson sheds light on a rich political experience of a Black activist in the early days of the Democratic Farmer Labor Party. David V. Taylor, a well-trained, professional historian has offered us a general and informative work on African Americans in St. Paul. His book speaks of a community from the 19th to 20th century, its origin and evolution as nurturing, caring and proud.

And now comes Arthur C. McWatt's sterling and unprecedented addition of the aptly titled, *Crusaders for Justice: A Chronicle of Protest by Agitators, Advocates and Activists in Their Struggle for Civil and Human Rights in St. Paul, 1802-1985*. The fact that McWatt has put together a strenuously researched narrative on the civil rights struggle in St. Paul, with clarity, strength and grace is only a part of its meaning and value. He has authored a seminal work, unmatched thus far, that will be endlessly useful to researchers and general interest readers for years to come. It represents, among other things, foundational and archival material. Further, it fills a void for a much needed document, if you will, or reference work, which tells the understudied and heretofore somewhat incoherent story of the role of Black people in St. Paul in the struggle for democracy.

By extension, the skillful pen of McWatt registers the history of African Americans in the state of Minnesota. His writing brings the creative edge of high historical drama to the fore. It is a script, which captures the stuff of life itself. The marvelous and the terrible, responses to challenges, heroism in the face of inhumanity, courage, persistence and hope, the critical events and small victories, as well as the soft, warm and beautiful side of human weight and complexity. He gives due diligence to what gives any people their respectively peculiar and beautiful humanity.

McWatt, a retired and widely respected history teacher who labored in the St. Paul public school system for more than three decades, articulates a moving and informing narrative of history. He begins with George Bonga and his offspring from his union with a Chippewa woman in the late 1700s. The emergence of Black presence in Minnesota predates that of all but the indigenous peoples of the land, and a handful of Frenchmen. Chronologically, this makes Black Minnesotans key witnesses to the evolution of Minnesota, from French predominance, from being part of Wisconsin Territory, to statehood in 1858, when Minnesota became officially part and parcel of the American Republic. McWatt establishes grounds for Blacks in the historical process, against trivial appearance by spontaneous combustion, as so much of Black American existence appears in the eyes of White Americans. He first grinds out the sweep of African American life from what was once the western frontier to pockets of modern urban community in St. Paul, the settling of Fort Snelling in the 1830s on the part of the U.S. government and its continuous expansion and acquisition of land. Urban life in Minnesota begins with the founding of the city of St. Paul and African Americans were at its embryonic state of development. The ambivalent relations between African and indigenous people is revealed.

A page is turned on the Dred Scott decision in 1857, the most compelling Supreme Court decision in pre-Civil war America. Dred Scott, an ordinary slave, brought to Minnesota territory as the manservant of Dr. John Emerson, became the cause celebré of the abolitionists when he sued for his freedom after returning to Missouri, a slave state. The court ruled against Scott and his supporters, the verdict disallowing any person of African descent to be a citizen of the United States. The Dred Scott case connects Minnesota and Black people to a major event, which led to the most dangerous period in American history -The Civil War. From here, the telling of this story runs the gamut, from A to Z. One is amazed to learn how deep and complex is the story of Africans in Minnesota, from territory to statehood.

Pioneering personalities such as James Thompson, an early settler in St. Paul, J.Q. Adams the journalist and forerunner of the protest tradition, and Robert Hickman, the founder of Pilgrim Baptist Church are cited as institution builders in 19th century Minnesota. Pilgrim Baptist Church (1863) is one of the oldest institutions in the state of Minnesota. He gives due recognition to white compatriots of Minnesota who believed in the cause of Black peoples' fight for social justice: the likes of John Ireland, Alexander Ramsey, Henry Rice, Bishop Whipple, and Charles Landrau are among the prominent white Minnesotans significantly acknowledged.

This kaleidoscopic view serves McWatt well. He seems to have grasped every critical detail regarding his *Crusaders for Justice*. The key struggles of Blacks from the acquisition of voting rights in 1868 to the founding of chapters of civil rights organizations, such as the National Association for the Advancement of Colored People, and newspapers such as The Western Appeal, and its giant editor J.Q. Adams, The Minneapolis Spokesman and St. Paul Recorder (now the Minnesota Spokesman-Recorder) and its fearless champion of civil and human rights, Cecil Newman.

McWatt stretches far and wide in gathering data and giving us impressions of a number of local personalities, some of who went to make contributions to the national struggle. Frederick McGhee, a brilliant lawyer, who was one of the founders of WE.B. Dubois's Niagara Movement, the fore runner to the NAACP. Also Roy Wilkins, the Executive Secretary of the National NAACP for 22 years, Whitney Young, who did graduate work at the University of Minnesota, later to become the Chief Officer of the National Urban League, and Carl Stokes who also did graduate work at the U of M before being elected, the first Black Mayor of a major American city, Cleveland, OH.

This book is good news, not only because it is timely, important and interesting, but also that it fills a need, not only for our community, but also for the American community (Black and white) at large. It is a primer for getting a handle on things. In short, McWatt has hit a home run clear out the park with the bases full.

Mahmoud El-Kati, Retired Professor, Macalester College

Contents

Dedication iii

Foreword v

Introduction xi

Acknowledgements xiii

One   1802 – 1849 1
George Bonga, James Thompson

Two   1850 – 1885 9
Robert T. Hickman
Governor William R. Marshall
Senator William Windom
U.S. Rep.Ignatius Donnelly

Three   1886 – 1899 21
Archbishop John Ireland
John Quincy (J.Q.) Adams
J. Frank Wheaton

Four   1900 –1919 31
Frederick L. McGhee, William T. Francis
Stephen L. Theobald

Five   1920 – 1929 53
The Duluth Lynching, Elmer Carter
Earl Wilkins

Six   1930 – 1939 71
Cecil Newman, Clifford Rucker
Clarence Mitchell, J. Louis Ervin
Reverend Francis J. Gilligan

Seven 1940 – 1949 99
S. Vincent Owens, Reverend T. R. Nelson
Whitney Young

Eight 1950 – 1959 127
Reverend Denzil Carty, Leonard Carter
Governor Luther Youngdahl

Nine 1960 – 1969 159
Clifford Rucker, Katie McWatt
Lawrence Borom, Allie Mae Hampton

Ten 1970 – 1979 187
Donald Lewis, Roy Wilkins
Mayor George Latimer, Bill Wilson

Epilogue **Early 1980s** 213
Mahmoud El-Kati
Nathaniel Abdul Khaliq
Reverend James W. Battle

Author's Biography 221

Arthur's Family Vignettes 28, 49, 184

Index 225

Bibliography 231

Photo Credits 235

Introduction

My interest in writing this book stems, in part, from the research I did on Minnesota history when I was a graduate student in the late 1950s and early 60s. I was impressed by the manner in which early African-American settlers like George Bonga and James Thompson had been accepted by many prominent Minnesota pioneers including Alexander Ramsey, Bishop Henry B. Whipple, Henry M. Rice, Charles E. Flandrau and the Reverends Alfred Brunson and Charles Hobart. My interest was further piqued when I discovered that officers and enlisted men from Minnesota's Civil War regiments had volunteered, in greater numbers than from any other state, in the Union, to lead the newly formed United States Colored Troops during the ensuing conflict.

In the period after the war, I admired the statesmanship of Governor William Marshall who supported and aided in bringing about the early enfranchisement of African-American males in Minnesota and also the efforts of Senator Windom and Representative Ignatius Donnelly to bring about a greater awareness to the Congress and the nation of the needs of the newly freed slaves. They were also among the few who called out to help the freedmen gain economic help and their civil rights.

After researching the early St. Paul African-American weeklies, beginning with their inception in the late nineteenth century, I decided to chronicle the struggles of these crusaders and champions from St. Paul in the hope that future generations might learn from what had transpired.

I soon discovered that though many of them had begun as local reporters, lawyers or political appointees, their impact had been felt not only in the city but often throughout the state and with some throughout the nation. Some had been crusaders while others were educators, agitators or advocates who informed, chided or even scolded their followers to act or who served as their mediators or surrogates in confrontations with authorities. At times they were conciliatory and other times argumentative but their effectiveness was often proven by their persistence in demanding equal rights for all and their ability to articulate citizens' needs.

Beginning with Editor J.Q. Adams, these champions carried on the protest tradition begun by John B. Russwurm and Samuel E. Cornish, and set the tone for the city's African-American community activists for the next century. Editors kept their readers aware of new developments in the struggle locally as well as other parts of the nation in the fight for human rights and equal justice. It was a struggle carried on without distinction of gender or race. It began with the biracial American Law Enforcement League and evolved to the equally biracial National Association for the Advancement of Colored People, who are still on the cutting edge of the struggle. It was supported by entrepreneurs, civil servants, the clergy, agency heads and community leaders. They came from all levels of society and their actions should be regarded with both pride and appreciation by those who believe that not knowing one's history dooms one to repeat mistakes. I have merely tried to present the events and results of a representative group with a profound appreciation for the quintessential contributions of Adams and Cecil Newman, Publisher of the Minneapolis Spokesman and St. Paul Recorder.

I want to thank all those who both encouraged and inspired me to pay tribute to these heroes and heroines. I wish to express my gratitude to Dr. Russell Fridley, former Director of the Minnesota Historical Society gave me both encouragement and support in my initial research. I am also appreciative of the encouragement I received from Professors Paul Murphy, David Noble and Clark Chambers, of the University of Minnesota's history department, who were such a valuable part of my learning. I would also like to thank Virginia Kunz, of the Ramsey County Historical Society, who encouraged me to continue my writing and gave me an opportunity to be published. Finally, I want to thank my loving wife Katie, for her inspiration and support which inspired me to put forth this effort.

Arthur C. McWatt

ACKNOWLEDGMENTS

I would like to express my gratitude and appreciation for interviews with Ivy and Josephine Hagen, Virginia Greene, Bert Carter, Jessie Miller, Monsignor Francis Gilligan, Cora Belle Banks, Kenneth Griswold, Donald Lewis Sr., Robert Patterson, Allie Mae Hampton, Janabelle Murphy-Taylor, Bradford Benner, Carl Weschke and the Reverend Kneely Williams, all of whom made valuable contributions on the role of the NAACP in St. Paul. I would also like to thank George Todd for his information on Dining Car Waiters' Local #516. Valuable information was also obtained on persons and events in St. Paul through interviews with James Murray and Stanley Williams. Both my wife and Theodore "Ted" Allen had valuable comments on the civil rights contributions of the St. Paul Urban League. James "Jim" Griffin was an invaluable resource for many civic events and personages in the city's past as were the contributions of Estyr Bradley Peake whose thirty-five years as a newspaper columnist helped to further clarify the relationships of past members of the Black community. Others who made significant contributions included Judge Stephen Maxwell and Professor David Taylor, whose Guide to Historical Sources for Blacks in Minnesota, provided both direction and inspiration for my research on the city's African-American community.

Chapter One
1802 – 1849

"Our blacks are attentive to their business and are no idlers. They are a useful class here on the confines of barbarism and do as much to put a civilized aspect on the force of society as any other class."

Editor James M. Goodhue, *Minnesota Pioneer, 1850*
St. Paul Recorder 6/6/1958

Perhaps the story of the African-American's role in Minnesota history really began in 1782 when U.S. Army Captain Daniel Robertson brought his slave, Jean Bonga to the Northwest Territory from Mackinac, Michigan. Jean was freed that year and on June 25th, 1794, he married a free African-American woman and continued his work with the Northwest Fur Company of Hudson Bay.[1] Almost a generation later, his son, Pierre, followed in his footsteps and went to work for Astor's American Fur Company, which had a post at Fort William on Lake Superior. Pierre married an Ojibway woman and in 1802, a son, George, was born in Duluth who was quite likely the state's first native-born African-American. Pierre prospered and sent his son to Montreal for his early education and upon his return Pierre found him conversant in French and English as well as his mother's language. It later resulted in his being pressed into service as an interpreter for Wisconsin Territorial Governor Lewis Cass in his crucial negotiations with the Sioux during the Treaty of Fond du Lac in 1820. George worked for his father and together they prospered and established trading posts at Crow Wing, Otter Tail and Cass counties as he grew into manhood.

As a young man, George Bonga was described by his contemporaries as being over six feet tall, powerfully built and on more than one occasion had proven his strength by portaging enormous amounts of goods. His skin texture was described as, "so black that it fairly glistened," but his naïveté about color was apparent even later in life when he astonished his friends by reminiscing, "Gentleman, I assure you that John Banfil and I were the first white men to ever come into this territory."[2]

George Bonga

His personal demeanor was described as gregarious, honest and fair in his relations with both immigrant and native populations. In one of his letters to State Senator Henry Rice, he spoke of his anxiety over the dishonesty of one of the Indian agents and his hope that rectitude would be forthcoming. In another letter he expressed concern over the fact that his trading license had been held up and suggested that if necessary the whole Crow Wing nation would go his bond. It is also evident from his personal correspondence that his association with Henry H. Sibley dates back to 1834 when Sibley had assumed command of the American Fur Company headquarters at St. Peter.

In 1837, Bonga assisted Wisconsin Territorial Governor Henry Dodge in his negotiations with over 1,200 Chippewa tribal members for lands on the St. Croix while sections of lands east of the river were being negotiated with the Sioux in Washington, D.C. The following year, Pierre "Pigs Eye" Parrant established a claim on those lands that later became the present site of St. Paul.

Bonga also carried on correspondence with Alexander Ramsey, historian, Charles Flandrau and leading Democrat Henry Rice.

When a message from Bonga warned Major Joseph Plympton, the commander of Fort Snelling, of an impending Indian uprising, Plympton told Bishop Whipple of his suspicions as to its veracity. Whipple assured him without hesitation, that, "No word could be better trusted than that of George Bonga!"[3]

In 1837, Bonga's reputation for bravery gained additional support with his pursuit and capture of Che-Ga-Wa-Skung, a Chippewa renegade, who was suspected of murdering Alfred Aitkin, the son of the head of the American Fur Company's Fond du Lac station. His capture was achieved only after a pursuit which lasted six days and five nights. It was the territory's first criminal trial, which ended up with the accused being acquitted.

In the aftermath, Bonga was threatened with reprisals, by some member of the suspect's tribe but fortunately they were never carried out. It still helped to make Bonga a hero and enhanced his persona and rustic charm; of which Flandrau wrote, his honesty; which had been praised by Bishop Whipple and his sagacity; ascribed to him by Senator Rice. His friendly relations with other traders, his role in the passage of historic treaties and the hospitality of his lodge all contributed to the favorable gifts he left to posterity. For the remainder of his life he continued to maintain trading posts at La Platte, Otter Tail and Leech Lakes and in 1880, he died at the age of seventy leaving his wife, Ashwinn and four children, who in turn, produced progeny who, by the end of the century, numbered well over one hundred. Following his death, the local populace named their township Bungo, in his honor for the many contributions he had made to both his county and his community.

During those early stages of settlement the avenues of entry for African-Americans were limited and had begun with a trickle of personal servants brought to Fort St. Anthony by southern officers who traditionally garrisoned the forts. The steamboat "Virginia" had arrived at Fort Snelling in 1823, and there appears to have been scant evidence of any trading in human beings taking place with the notable exception of the sale of a slave girl to Dr. John Emerson, who was stationed there temporarily in 1836. Emerson had bought Harriet Robinson to be the wife of Dred Scott, whom he had bought from Elizabeth Blow when he had been stationed in Richmond, Virginia.[4]

A second African-American pioneer who created a positive climate of opinion in the state's early frontier history was James Thompson, a slave, who had been born in Virginia in 1809, and who was owned by George Monroe, the nephew of the former President, who brought him to Kentucky only to loan him to John Culbertson who brought him to Fort Snelling in 1827. There Culbertson attempted to sell him to a Captain Day who discovered his true ownership and laid claim to him for a past debt which Monroe had owed him.[5] Day kept Thompson at Fort Snelling where he was allowed to mingle with another group of slaves from his home state that had been brought there by Colonel Zachary Taylor, an officer who was later to become the nation's twelfth President and who, in 1849, would appoint Alexander Ramsey as the state's first territorial governor. When he was later re-assigned, Day took Thompson to Fort Crawford, near Prairie du Chien, where he allowed him to marry a Sioux woman and Thompson soon became conversant in her language.

On May 2, 1837, the Reverend Alfred Brunson, a Methodist missionary, arrived in the newly designated Wisconsin Territory to minister to the needs of the native population and sought out Thompson to serve as his interpreter at his Kaposia Mission. In order to gain Thompson's freedom, Brunson found it necessary to write some friends in Cincinnati, Ohio, and suggest they advertise in the Western Christian Advocate to raise the necessary $1,200 to purchase him. After the funds were raised, Brunson magnanimously presented Thompson with his free papers.[6]

Thompson was described as a tall, slender man with aquiline features, a light complexion and an angular build. While serving at the mission he managed to improve his skills as a carpenter and became a fluent interpreter as well as a zealous Christian. The mission managed to maintain itself despite a number of bloody skirmishes between the Sioux and the Ojibway which were finally settled by the Battle of Kaposhia, after which the mission was moved to St. Paul.

4

In 1838, Thompson helped Edward Phelan, a recently discharged veteran, build a house near what is now known as Seven Corners, on the outskirts of the St. Paul's downtown area.[7]

Shortly after this generous act, it appears that Thompson became intemperate in his use of alcohol, which resulted in an incident which became known as, "The Tournament of Seven Corners" and was accused, by Phelan, of stealing a pig. Though Thompson was eventually exonerated, his reputation suffered.

Also during this period he decided to open a whiskey shop opposite Fort Snelling, which caused him to incur the wrath of the military authorities as well as being branded by the city's religious leaders as having abandoned his Christian principles.

However, he regained public favor and by 1846, was praised in an editorial in the Minnesota Pioneer for his business acumen and rumors circulated that he had once owned all the land south of Ninth Street, between Minnesota and Robert Streets, which extended south to the river.[8]

The following year the platting of St. Paul's Lowertown was completed by surveyors Ira and Benjamin Brunson, and Thompson improved his public image by donating 2,000 feet of lumber and 1,500 roofing shingles as well as money toward the construction of the territory's first Methodist mission, which was located between Market and St. Peter Streets. Its founding members included C. Leader, the Reverend Close, Mr. and Mrs. F. Hoy, a Mr. J. Hoffman, a Miss Sarah McCann, two members of the Biefansky family and James Thompson. The mission was officially chartered on December 31, 1848.[9]

Later in life, Thompson continued to have bouts of intemperance but also gained a reputation as a dependable guide who led a number of hunting parties throughout the territory and had also operated the area's first ferry boat. He served the community for many years and with the exception of his son, Charles, survived eight of his nine children. He also had the distinction of being the only African-American member of the Minnesota's Old Settlers Club. He and his wife died in Nebraska, in 1884.[10]

During the first half of the 19th century few African-Americans entered the unorganized territories that Minnesota was a part of despite the fact there were no laws that restricted their migration and public sentiment was largely anti-slavery. Throughout this period Minnesota remained part of seven different territorial entitles until it gained its own status in 1858. The following year the Census listed only 59 African-Americans in the entire state with over half of its nine organized counties containing none.

The French Canadians, with whom Bonga was familiar and spoke their language, tended to accept African-Americans who were able to assimilate themselves into their culture. They admired Bonga, both for his business acumen as well as his skills as a trapper. Thompson was also admired, by many, for his language skills and his success as an artisan. Both contributed to the state's heritage and folk-lore, particularly to Cass and Ramsey counties, though the entire state was richer as a result of their contributions. Neither of them made a direct impact on the impending struggle for civil rights in the state's Capitol but together they helped lay the foundations for future dialogues between the races by creating respect between themselves and some of the states' early religious and civic leaders of both the territory and state.

CHAPTER ONE BIBLIOGRAPHY

1. "Negroes in the Fur Trade," Kenneth W. Porter, *Minnesota History*, Volume XV, December 1934, pp. 421–433

2. *St. Paul Recorder*, 28 March 1958.

3. "Letters of George Bonga," *Journal of Negro History*, January 1927, pp. 41–54.

4. Low, Augustus and Clift, Virgil A., *Encyclopedia of Black America*, McGraw Hill Book Company, New York, 1981, p. 748.

5. St. Paul Recorder, 27 May 1949.

6. Hiran, Steven, "Slavery in Minnesota," *History of the Bench and Bar*, Chapter III, pp. 30–31.

7. Spangler, Earl, *The Negro in Minnesota*, Y.S. Denison and Company Publishers, Minneapolis, MN., 1961, p. 20.

8. *St. Paul Dispatch*, 5 October 1906.

9. "The Negro Population in Minneapolis," Abram Harris, *Minneapolis Urban League and Phyllis Wheatley House Report*, 1926.

10. Brunson, Ella C. "Alfred Brunson, Pioneer of Wisconsin Methodists," *Winona Magazine of History*, Volume IV, No. 2, December 1918, p. 12.

Chapter Two
1850 – 1885

"Education is our passport to the future, for tomorrow belongs to those who prepare for it today."

Malcolm X

During the 1854 territorial legislative session, some anti-black sentiment arose with the introduction in the House, a "Black Code" bill which would have required African-Americans to post a $300 to $500 bond to guarantee their good behavior. It was defeated 10-6 in a committee vote.[1] An attempt was also made in 1857 to segregate African-American school children in a Lowertown school taught by a Moses Dixon, which closed shortly after its opening.

In August of 1865, the St. Paul School Board established another "School for Colored Children," which opened in the Morrison Building, which was taught by a Miss Morrow, and though it began with 40 African-American students by January 1868 only 20 were still in attendance in the dilapidated facility. By November, voters approved Suffrage for "Afro-males, Indians and Mixed-Bloods" and the following March 4th ended segregation of schools and two days later six of the African-American students integrated the newly constructed Franklin Elementary School.[2]

In 1864, during his first session as a U.S. Representative, Ignatius Donnelly boldly declared, "We must regenerate the South and plant a free press firmly on its soil and we must enforce equal education upon both blacks and whites."[9]

Though Donnelly echoed the sentiments of many African-Americans in St. Paul, the reality was apparent the following year when the *St. Paul Daily Press* reported on "The dilapidated room, in the Morrison

9

Building which is being called Adams School for Negroes which has broken windows, falling plaster and few school supplies."[10]

During this period, African-American children in the Lake Como area were also facing discrimination in both their religious and public school instruction. Copperheads there had ousted their Sunday School Superintendent Potts for integrating "colored" and white students and had insisted that the students be taught separately. Their mandate was signed both by officials from St. Paul and the trustees of Rose town.[11] The Copperheads were a vocal group of white Democrats in the Northern United States Union who opposed the American Civil War and wanted an immediate peace settlement with the Confederates.

It was also about this time that Minnesotan's elected Republican William R. Marshall as Governor. He had been both a publisher of the *St. Paul Daily Press* and a University of Minnesota Regent.

The war had begun auspiciously for the state when Territorial Governor Ramsey became the first northern leader to volunteer one thousand men, of the state's militia, to the Union cause on April 12, 1861. With the passage of the Militia Act of July 17, 1862, 104 African-American men, or almost half of the state's 1860 Census total, responded to the call to serve with the newly formed U.S. Colored Troops.[12] It was also to the state's credit that its Third, Fourth and Seventh Regiments recruited a large number of volunteers who offered their services as leaders of the colored troops. Colonel Levine P. Plummer, of the Third Regiment, volunteered to lead the 72nd U.S. Colored Infantry Regiment. Lieutenant Wesly Miller fell at the Battle of Gettysburg leading a company of colored troops. Minnesota's Fourth Regiment offered the services of 18 officers to help train and command African-American recruits. Second Lieutenant William Wells was given command of the Colored 69th Regiment while the Reverend Enos Minger volunteered to serve as Chaplain for the regiment. Altogether, 72 white Minnesotans volunteered to lead U.S. Colored Troops.[13]

Early in 1867, Minnesota's U.S. Representative Ignatius L. Donnelly again stepped forward to champion the needs of the newly freed slaves when he submitted a resolution to the Congress to make a Committee on Education a permanent standing committee with admonition that, "Universal education must go hand in hand with universal suffrage."[14]

Earlier in that decade, a third prominent African-American settler arrived in Minnesota. He was Robert T. Hickman, who was born in Boone County, Missouri, on January 1, 1830. In his youth, he often was assigned the task of rail-splitting on a plantation in Clayville where he was held in bondage. Fortunately, a benevolent master taught him how to read and write and after studying the Bible extensively, he was allowed to occasionally preach, to other slaves on the plantation. During the time he was in bondage, he married an enslaved woman named Mindy who subsequently bore him a son, John, and a daughter, Edith.

One night in May 1863, he and his family, with the help of Union troops, were allowed to steal away and join a larger group who had also been freed. As they made their way north they were joined by other freed slaves and their group soon swelled to over three hundred. Half of them were directed to board the steamer, War Eagle, to begin their journey north.

Robert Hickman

As they made their way up the Mississippi, the steamer stopped at Davenport, Iowa, where 32 of the able-bodied former slaves volunteered to join the 60th United States Colored Infantry Regiment, many of whose members, after the war, went on to lobby for the equal rights of African-Americans. By 1868, they had helped win the vote for African-Americans in that state.[3]

Upon their approach to St. Paul's Landing, the sight of African-Americans on the decks brought forth a volley of threats and curses from those who lined the docks. The contrabands (former slaves) soon realized that they may have been recruited to break a prolonged strike of Irish dock workers which had been called against the St. Paul and Galena Packet Company. Finding it impossible to disembark in St. Paul, the captain ordered his crew to let some of the contrabands ashore on the southern bank near Fort Snelling and St. Anthony while others headed south to Blue Earth Country.

Shortly after their arrival the Democratic-oriented St. Paul Pioneer editorialized that, "We understand that the War Eagle has brought up a cargo of 150 niggers and 150 mules on government account. It plans to take back some eight or nine hundred Indians. We doubt very much whether we will benefit by the exchange. If we had our way, we would send both the niggers and the Indians to Missouri and keep the mules."[4]

During the week following their arrival many of Hickman's followers re-congregated in St. Paul and held religious services. The Republican owned *St. Paul Daily Press* commented editorially, "That our new arrivals have recently made an application to rent some lodge rooms at the Good Templar to hold religious services, once or twice a week. They are furnishing further proof of the superiority over their Kilkenny persecutors by the favorable contrast of their quiet, civil and inoffensive manners, with the brutal insolence of the savages who assailed them with insults and even bodily violence, upon their arrival."[5]

Hickman's followers finally found a church building on Twelfth and St. Peter Streets where prayer services could be held. After two months of planning, the group obtained mission status, from First Baptist Church of St. Paul. The following January, Hickman and fifteen other members began writing to prominent Baptist groups, telling them they were not satisfied with their status and would like to become a branch.[6]

CHAPTER TWO 1850 - 1885

By 1866, Hickman had succeeded in formally organizing Pilgrim Baptist with the help of Fielding Combs, Henry Moffitt, John Trotter and Giles Crenshaw.

They celebrated the occasion by baptizing new members on the shores of the Mississippi River.[7] The young congregation arranged for the purchase of a $200 lot on the corner of Sibley and Morris Streets on which they erected a church built of stone and wood, which had a seating capacity of 300. The $2,400 building costs were paid by First Baptist Church who continued to exercise their control by appointing a white pastor, William Norris, while relegating Hickman to the role of clerk though they did allow him to represent the church at their annual denominational meetings.

In 1868, Andrew Torbet, a Scottish immigrant, was assigned to Pilgrim Baptist and served until 1874 when Hickman was finally licensed to preach and was granted his ordination the following year.[8] In 1878, he became the congregation's official minister and used his newly acquired authority to found Zion Mission in Minneapolis.

Succeeding Reverend Hickman was the Reverend Bird J. Wilkins, who during his pastorate secured a lot for $12,000 on the corner of Summit and Cedar Street where a third church was built that housed what soon became the city's largest African-American Baptist congregation.

Following the armistice, when Marshall became Governor, he led his party to propose the right to vote for all adult males in the state. The referendum they offered the voters went down in defeat by a margin of 2,513 of the 27,789 votes cast.

During his second term, Marshall's proposal again went down to defeat but in the fall of 1868 a compromise was reached with the Democrats. In return for an easy-amending process to the state's constitution, the Democrats agreed to permit all-male suffrage. Marshall signed the measure making Minnesota one of the first states in the Union to give African-American males the right to vote.[15]

Shortly after the bill became law, Edmund James, Ralph Grey and J.K. Hilyard were major participants in sponsoring a state convention of the Sons of Freedom for the New Year. On January 1, 1869, Governor Marshall mounted the platform to address the assembled delegates, "I welcome you all to liberty and equality before the law. In the name of the state of Minnesota, which has relieved itself of the reproach of unjust discrimination against a class of its people, I welcome you to your political enfranchisement!"[16]

In the fall, a bill was introduced in the Minnesota legislature making school segregation illegal. It was passed by a 30 to 12 vote in the Senate and a lesser majority in the House. Governor Marshall signed it into law on March 3, 1869. It simply stated, "that school authorities were not to classify or separate children on the basis of color, social position or nationality or the State Superintendent of Education would thereafter withhold state funds from such schools which failed to comply."[17]

Three days after President Grant's inauguration, in March 1869, African-American activists, in St. Paul, pushed for their right to serve on juries and were rewarded on March 25th with the appointment of R.A. Stockton, M. Jernigan, Henry Moffit, Thomas Jackson and Robert Hickman were sworn in to serve as St. Paul's first African-American jurors in a municipal court. The occasion was the trial of an African-American in the Court of Common Pleas.

During the 1870s, both U.S. Senator William Windom and U.S. Representative Ignatius Donnelly served as advocates for the rights of African-Americans, both locally and nationally. Windom continued to warn his fellow Republicans that, "The color question is the most difficult problem now facing America!"[18] At Windom's funeral, Donnelly lauded him for his wisdom and compassion and declared, "His sagacity, intuition and humanity will always remain imperishable to Minnesota's heritage and are gifts which will neither be ignored nor forgotten."[19]

A third public figure who spoke out for the rights of St. Paul's African-American community was John Ireland. Ireland was born in Kilkenny, Ireland, on September 11, 1838. On May 20, 1852, his parents arrived on the steamboat Nominee at the Jackson Street Levee with him and his five siblings. John's father, who was a carpenter and his friend John O'Gorman built a temporary home for their two families on Fifth and St. Peter Streets. Later a permanent Ireland home was built on West Fifth between Market and Washington, which is the present site of the St. Paul Main Library. It was a neighborhood which had a fair number of African-American neighbors as the local Census of 1865 listed nine colored families on the same page as the Irelands.

When John was 15 years of age, he was selected by Bishop Cretin to study for the priesthood and after completing his seminary training, he was sent to Rome for graduate studies.

Upon his return, he found the country in the midst of the Civil War. At the urging of Bishop Grace, Ireland was appointed as an auxiliary chaplain to minister to the spiritual needs of the Catholics in Minnesota's Fifth Regiment.[20] After only ten months of service, Ireland was mustered out and it appears from this memoirs that the highlight of his tour of duty came during the Fifth's stand at the Battle of Corinth, Mississippi. During the heat of that battle some of the troops found themselves running low on ammunition and the young chaplain hurried down the battle line carrying ammunition and shouting, "Here are your cartridges boys, don't spare them!"[21] In later years, he sometimes romanticized about the battle in an oft-repeated syllogism which suggested that since the Fifth had prevented Confederate General Rosecrans from surrounding Union forces at Corinth and prevented a disastrous defeat, it necessarily followed that the Fifth had really saved the Union.

Ireland always managed somehow to either play down or simply ignore the Battle of Nashville which many historians gave far greater significance to in the ending of the South's resistance. It was in that engagement that the Minnesota 5th, 7th, 9th and 10th Regiments fought gallantly. Despite heavy losses they succeeded in forcing open the back door of the Confederacy, which allowed Union forces to march into the heartlands of the South.[22]

After the war the young priest was often seen instructing African-American converts in the old brick schoolhouse on Sixth and Wabasha, which perhaps later inspired him to speak out boldly upon their behalf.

Also at this time in 1868, Governor Marshall joined 18 of the other 37 state governors who had extended African-American men the right to vote.[23] Political apathy, however, still marked most Republican attitudes toward the 180 African-Americans counted in the city census. Most concern was given to matters such as the regulation of railroads, combating locusts and economic development rather than any thought of civil rights. The skills that many African-Americans had brought with them from the South were largely ignored by the local populace, almost half of whom had their roots, as well as their prejudices, firmly planted there. African-Americans were banned from the skilled trades and were forced to find their employment in service for domestic occupations.

In 1873, Frederick Douglass visited St. Paul, as a guest of the Atheneum Association, to celebrate the anniversary of the Emancipation Proclamation. The occasion was saddened, however, when the Village of White Bear refused to allow the celebrants to use their public park and Douglass had to speak at the Pence Opera House.

In 1875, African-American Henry W. Robinson was denied the right to even purchase a first class ticket by the Milwaukee and St. Paul Railway Company. He brought suit at the Federal District Court for $1,800 damages but the jury decided in favor of the defendant.[24]

CHAPTER TWO 1850 - 1885

A decade later the U.S. Supreme Court dealt all African-Americans a severe blow when they ruled that the Civil Rights Act of 1875, "violated an owner's right to private property when by requiring proprietors to admit black patrons to their places of public accommodations." The nine Republican Justices who made up the court also ruled that, "state legislatures and not the Congress or a Federal District Court had the sole jurisdiction over citizens' rights." This reinforced the "State Rights" doctrine and sanctioned the further brutalization of African-Americans that had begun after the election of President Rutherford B. Hayes in 1876. Frederick Douglass noted that, "It came upon the country like a clap of thunder from a clear sky," and he sadly noted that only Justice Harlan, who ironically was the only one of the Justices who had been a slave-holder, had stood up for the rights of "colored" citizens as they were defined by the Fourteenth Amendment to the Constitution.[25]

By the dawn of the 1880s, however, the fourth estate and its Protest Tradition was destined to rise to a new level of leadership in St. Paul, with the advent of the First Crusader for Justice.

CHAPTER TWO BIBLIOGRAPHY

1. Spangler, Earl, *The Negro in Minnesota*, p. 27.

2. "Race and Segregation in St. Paul's Schools: 1846–69, William D. Green, *Minnesota History*, Winter 1996–97, p. 144–146.

3. Glatthaar, Joseph T., *Forged in Battle: The Civil War Alliance of Black Soldiers and White Officers*, The Free Press, New York City, 1990, p.250.

4. *St. Paul Pioneer,* 6 May 1863.

5. *St. Paul Daily Press*, 16 May 1863.

6. Baptist Papers Correspondence (1853-1889), 17 January 1864, Minnesota Historical Society Collection.

7. Minutes of the Board of Trustees; First Baptist Church of St. Paul, 13 November 1866.

8. Minutes of the Minnesota Baptist State Convention, pp, 82–83.

9. *Ignatius Donnelly in Congress*, Thesis by Kenneth Hall, Minnesota Historical Society,15 July 1959, p. 10.

10. Spangler, Earl, *The Negro in Minnesota*, p. 34.

11. ibid., p. 35.

12. ibid., p. 25.

13. Glatthaar, Joseph T., *Forged in Battle: The Civil War Alliance of Black Soldiers and White Officers*, Macmillian Publishers, New York, 1990, p. 56.

14. *Congressional Globe*, 39th Congress, 1st Session, p. 590.

15. Author's Note: The Fifteenth Amendment to the U.S. Constitution was not ratified until March 30, 1870.

16. *The Negro in Minnesota*, p. 58.

17. *St. Paul Recorder,* 19 October 1956.

18. Windom's prophecy was reiterated by W.E.B. DuBois in the opening line of The Souls of Black Folks, when he noted, "The problem of the twentieth century is the problem of the color line."

19. *Minneapolis Tribune*, 14 February 1949.

20. Marvin R. O'Connell, John Ireland and the American Catholic Church, Minnesota Historical Society, St. Paul, 1988, p. 84. Shortly after his regiment was deployed to the South, regular Chaplain, James E. Chafee, took sick and Ireland was sent to replace him on June 23, 1862.

21. Moynihan, James H., T*he Life of Archbishop John Ireland*, Harper and Brothers Publishers, New York City, N.Y., 1953, p. 6.

22. Kenneth Carly, *Minnesota in the Civil War*, Ross and Haines Incorporated, Minneapolis, MN, The four Minnesota regiments lost 302 men. Ireland, in re-shaping the war's history often slighted the contributions of the gallant Minnesota First Regiment, at Gettysburg who had the largest one day loss of any, Union regiment during the entire war. Their valor gave President Lincoln the courage to issue his preliminary Emancipation Proclamation and their brave repulse of Pickett's Charge changed the course of the war.

23. Green, William D., "Minnesota's Long Road to Black Suffrage: 1849-1868." *Minnesota History*, 56/2 Summer 1998, p. 84.

24. *St. Paul Dispatch*, 17 May 1875.

25. William S. McFeely, *Frederick Douglas*, W.W. Norton and Company, New York City, 1991, pp. 318–19.

Chapter Three
1886 – 1899

"If there is no struggle, there is no progress. Those who profess to favor freedom and yet deprecate agitation are men who want crops without plowing up the ground. They want rain without thunder and lightning. They want oceans without the awful roar of its many waters. The struggle may be a moral one; or it may be a physical one; or it may be both moral and physical; but it must be a struggle…"

Frederick Douglass

Along with the advent of the St. Paul, Minneapolis and Manitoba Railway came the gradual utilization of the Twin City's African-American population. This railway evolved into James J. Hill's Great Northern System, which began by recruiting waiters and porters from Chicago, but soon found a local work force waiting and willing in the Twin Cities. The 1890 Census had listed 3,683 African-Americans in Minnesota with only a fourth of them being native-born and over half from the South. In 1885, the *Western Appeal* had been sold to Thomas H. Lyles and James K. Hilyard of St. Paul. Lyles owned a large barber-shop and was a realtor as well as a mortician while Hilyard was a musician and a tailor and owned a cleaning and renovating business at 486 Robert Street. Lyles had not only been instrumental in the passage of the state's first Civil Rights Law that year, but had also been helpful in getting African-American L.W. Thomas appointed to the police force in 1881. He and his editor, F.D. Parker, were successful in convincing Mayor Rice to organize a "colored" fire company in 1884 and to appoint William R. Godette the following year, to head it. Though the civil rights thrust begun by Lyles was greatly appreciated by the African-American community, the *Appeal's* circulation continued to lag, and the owners finally decided to bring in John (J.Q.) Adams as its associate editor in an attempt to boost sales. Adams had been working as the editor of the Louisville Bulletin and had a good reputation as both a journalist and writer. He had been born on May 4, 1849, in Louisville, and had received his early education in private schools in both Fond du Lac, Wisconsin and in Yellow Springs, Ohio. After the Civil War, he served in a number of positions in the Freedmen's Bureau. While serving on the paper, he also worked as a bailiff in a St. Paul Municipal Court beginning in 1886. The following year, he became the sole editor of the *Appeal* and the principal stockholder of the Northwestern Publishing Company. In 1889, he dropped the word Western from the paper's masthead and began publishing five editions, in St. Paul, Chicago, Louisville, St. Louis and Dallas.

When he arrived, Adams found a city in which shops and businesses denied citizens of color the opportunity to use the skills they had acquired in the South, and parodied them with the same verses that had been used against Irish-Catholics a few decades earlier.

> Shame on the lips that utter it,
> Shame on the hands that write,
> Shame on the pages that publish it,
> Such slander to the light.
> I feel by blood with lightning speed,
> Through all my veins fast fly,
> At that old taunt, forever new,
> No Negroes (Irish) need Apply!

In 1888, when Archbishop Ireland had established the St. Peter Claver Mission, the Irish Standard noted that the Catholic church and Cardinal Gibbons had recently set apart the first Sunday of Lent as a day on which a collection should be taken up to furnish the means necessary for the evangelization of the colored people. The new mission was in the old Swedenborgian Church, which James Thompson had helped to build on the original Market Street site between Fourth, and Fifth and it had the distinction of being the first place of worship in St. Paul that had electric lights.[1]

In June, prior to a concert at Cretin Hall, Ireland spoke extemporaneously to three hundred whites and one hundred African-Americans and told them, "We are all brothers in Christ and brothers do not look at color or race. This country represents the human race and all colors are together. I believe it a providential design to show that all men are children of the same God."[2]

Ireland had Father John Shanley organize the mission during a period prior to Shanley's consecration as Bishop on December 27, 1889.

Frederick L. McGhee, who had moved to St. Paul that year and was of the Methodist faith, became so impressed by Shanley's advocacy that he switched faiths and told friends, "It was mainly due to Father Shanley that the rights of my people are being recognized." In 1890, Shanley along with Father Augustus Tolton, an African-American priest who had been ordained in Rome in 1886, wrote a weekly newsletter which appeared in the *Appeal*, persuaded Father John Gmeiner to present a series of lectures at St. Thomas College debunking false racial theories. At that time, St. Thomas was one of only two Catholic colleges in the United States which admitted African-American students.

In a January 1, 1891 Emancipation Day address, given at the St. Paul Armory to the Afro-American League, Ireland continued to plead the cause for human rights as he declared to the assembled crowd, "What do I claim for the black man? That which I claim for the white man, neither more nor less. I would blot out the color line….I would break down all barriers and let the Negro be our equal before the law. There are states where the violation of the Negro's most sacred personal rights secures impunity before the law. In many states the law forbids marriage between white and black, in this manner fomenting immorality and put-

Archbishop Ireland

ting injury no less upon the white whom it pretends to elevate than upon the black for whose degradation it has no care. I would in all public gatherings and in all public resorts, in halls and hotels, treat the black man as I treat the white. I might shun the vulgar man, whatever his color, but the gentleman, I would not dare push away from me."[3]

Writing to the Third Colored Catholic Congress, in 1892, Ireland told them, "So far as the diocese of St. Paul is concerned, my ideas are very decided that no distinction should be made as to the color of pupils in parish schools."[4]

Also that year, Father Edward Casey was chosen to be St. Peter Claver's first resident pastor and served for three years before he was succeeded by Father Thomas Printon who purchased the first parish rectory.

African-American editors in the Twin Cities were cognizant of the Catholic Church's position on race and in 1896, P.O. Gray, of the *World*, editorialized that "there is one very strong point in favor of bringing the Negro into the Catholic church which our Protestant brothers have been winking at for two hundred years and that is when a man or woman enters the Catholic church, he or she enters clothed with all the rights of everyone else, regardless of race or color."[5]

J.M. Griffin, editor of the *Afro-American Advance*, concurred when he wrote, "Too much praise cannot be given to the Catholic institutions of America in their attitude toward the Negro race. They have always ignored color lines. But such cannot be said of Protestant institutions." Griffin warned that, "The universal demand, of the hour, by intelligent and progressive Negroes, is an educated ministry ... We want men of learning who can expound the doctrine of the Bible to scientific men with the same effect as to those men who read no other book but the Bible."[6]

Adams suggested that perhaps, "The chief problem with the Negro appeared to be his lack of rebellion." He noted, "He often lacks the eternal dissatisfaction and the everlasting assertion that, 'I'm as good as you! Or if I am not my children will be!'"[7]

J. Q. Adams

His early militancy was also evident in another editorial published later that year which suggested that when African-Americans are finally forced to conclude that there is no possibility in this country for them to receive anything like justice or they are forced by circumstance to that conclusion, many will learn to sell their lives dearly. He suggested that if a man knew he was about to die at the hands of a merciless mob he should kill as many of its members as possible. This idea was a precursor of Claude McKay's sentiments in his famous Black Renaissance poem written three decades later, "If We Must Die."

Rival editor Griffin noted also that though Adams sometimes proclaimed his paper's non-partisanship he nevertheless went so far in one editorial to facetiously suggest that since Democrats had played the game of hide and seek so often with issues effecting colored people it might be prudent for colored men who want the best men elected, to vote for even bad Republicans if they wish their safety to be insured.

In 1890, the African-American population of Minnesota continued to face discrimination in housing as well as employment. Editor J. M. Griffin, in an editorial in the *Afro-American Advance*, noted "that our colored citizens' universal grievance comes from the difficulty with which the most respectable families find in renting a decent house in a desirable location. There is no justification for the emphatic manner in which local rental agents turn down and humiliate colored applicants for a house advertised to rent even though the tendency seems to be slightly better here than in Minneapolis."[8]

An interesting sidelight during this last decade of the century was the prominence of members of the legal profession on the staffs of local African-American weeklies. Lawyers J.M. Griffin and J.C. Reid published the Twin-City American. Their paper soon merged with the Colored Citizen published by another lawyer named J.L. Curtis and Mrs. George Duckett. Reid founded the Colored Citizen Publishing Company and the two papers combined to form the *Afro-American Advance*. All were vigorous in their protests and vigilant in their defense of civil liberties.

The person who truly made a difference in the rights of African-Americans in Minnesotan to protest was John Francis Wheaton, who was born in Hagerstown, Maryland, on May 8, 1866. After attending public schools there, he was sent to the state normal school at Harpers Ferry, West Virginia, to continue his education and graduated from there in 1882 as its valedictorian. He then attended Storer College in West Virginia before transferring to Howard University where he studied pre-law and graduated in 1892. The following year he came to Minnesota and entered the University of Minnesota Law School where he graduated in 1894 as its class orator. In 1895, he became Assistant Reading Clerk of the Minnesota House of Representatives and, in 1896, he became the first African-American to represent Minnesota at a Republican National Convention.

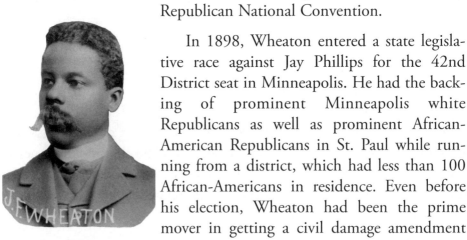

In 1898, Wheaton entered a state legislative race against Jay Phillips for the 42nd District seat in Minneapolis. He had the backing of prominent Minneapolis white Republicans as well as prominent African-American Republicans in St. Paul while running from a district, which had less than 100 African-Americans in residence. Even before his election, Wheaton had been the prime mover in getting a civil damage amendment

J. F. Wheaton

26

added to the 1885 civil rights bill to cover additional kinds of businesses. Soon after his election, he met with Governor David M. Clough to
demand that African-American soldiers from Minnesota, be made eligible for commissions in the Spanish-American War.[9] In the legislature his
brilliant oratory earned him the title of the "Demosthenes of the
Northwest" and during his single term he succeeded, with the help of
attorneys Charles Scrutchin, William Morris and labor activist, Charles
E. James, in writing a second amendment to the Civil Rights Law which
closed a "saloon loophole" in the bill which had been opened in 1899,
by the case of Rhone vs. Loomis. He managed to have it pass in the
House by a slim majority, but in the senate, he obtained a large majority of 37 to 11. It was signed into law by Governor William H. Eustis
on March 6, 1899. Fred McGhee, however, withheld his support for the
changes because of his objections to both its new reduction in penalties
as well as its more lenient provisions for civil damages which had been
necessary to assure its passage.[10]

The decade drew to a close with the strong voices of Adams,
Wheaton, McGhee and future Trades and Labor President, James, continuing to be raised as officers of the newly formed Afro-American Law
Enforcement League of Minnesota whose main purposes were to defend
the civil and human rights of African-Americans. The group voted with
the local chapter of the National Afro-American Council to send finan-
cial aid to New Orleans to help in the prosecution of the fight against
the Louisiana Disfranchisement Law, which had been enacted near the
turn of the century.[11]

Family Heritage Vignette

My maternal grandparents were among the new arrivals. My grandmother, Martha Hill, was born in 1870, in Grenada, Mississippi, the offspring of a former slave and a Chickasaw woman who later moved to Holly Springs where she received her early education. She met Arthur Lowe in the mid 1880s who convinced her to return with him to his home in Nashville where she enrolled in his sister's school, Catherine Lowe's School for Colored Girls, and trained to become a teacher. They were soon married and started a family near the end of the decade.

My mother, Carrie, was born on December 23rd, 1889, and had been preceded by a brother, Arthur, and a sister, Bridie. During the next decade the family made their way up the Mississippi River, to St. Paul where my grandmother's schooling enabled them to acquire a considerable amount of land, most of which they sold to open Lowe's Art and Picture Framing Shop on Wabasha Street in the mid 1890s. The business flourished and by 1900 they were able to build a new home on Sherburne Ave.

By this time my mother's family had grown with the addition of three sisters, Ethel, Rebecca and Bessie and a younger brother Freddie. Their good fortune was marred shortly after their move by the death of Freddie from typhoid fever only ten days after their arrival in their new home on August 28th.

CHAPTER THREE BIBLIOGRAPHY

1. *St. Paul Recorder*, 13 May 1949. Excerpts from, "The Story of Early Catholic Efforts in behalf of state Negroes."

2. ibid..

3. *St. Paul Recorder*, 20 May 1949.

4. *St. Paul Recorder*, 27 May 1949.

5. *Negro World*, 19 December 1896.

6. *Afro-American Advance*, 17 February 1900.

7. *Appeal*, 17 May 1903.

8. *Twin City American*, 4 May 1899.

9. Spangler, Earl, *The Negro in Minnesota*, T.S. Denison and Company, Minneapolis, 1961, p. 70.

10. Nelson, Paul D., *Frederick L. McGhee; A Life on the Color Line: 1861-1912*, Minnesota Historical Society, St. Paul, Minnesota, 2002. pp. 56-57.

11. *Afro-American Advance*, 31 March 1900.

Chapter Four
1900 – 1919

"To sin by silence, when we should protest makes cowards of us all. The human race has climbed on protest and had no voice been raised against injustice, ignorance would serve the law and the guillotine would decide the least dispute. The few who dare must speak again, to right the wrongs of those whose tongues are still."

Ella Wheeler Wilcox, Appeal, 12 January 1918

Perhaps the most dominant local advocate of the civil rights tradition in the first decade of the twentieth century was Frederick L. McGhee. McGhee was born on October 28, 1861, in Monroe County, Mississippi, of slave parents. After the emancipation, he and his father Abraham, who was a blacksmith, and his mother, Sarah, moved to Knoxville, Tennessee. There, Frederick briefly attended a Presbyterian elementary school before being orphaned in 1873. He then attended a high school for a short period, which was paid for by the Freedmen Bureau, but he gained most of his education in the subsequent two years he spent at Knoxville College.

In 1879, he went to Chicago where he began to read the law and in 1885 he managed to graduate from the Northwestern University School of Law and joined the practice of Edward H. Morris.

He came to St. Paul in 1889 with his wife Mattie and soon became the first African-American lawyer to practice before the Minnesota Supreme Court. He located his law office on Union Block near the Union Depot where his practice soon prospered.

He was a militant and effective champion for civil rights and helped form the Afro-American League of St. Paul in 1889. He also brought suits against proprietors who discriminated against African-Americans. Perhaps one of his most important contributions was his broadening of the social consciousness of African-American citizens. He was one of the first to recognize that party loyalty should be secondary to the fight against racism. Even before his break with the Republican Party, in 1892, he urged blacks to vote the interests of their race rather than those of their party. The estrangement with the Republicans came about when his appointment as a Presidential Elector was challenged by a Scandinavian faction of the Republican Party who resented his receiving the honor but under the false pretext that he had been delinquent in his party fees. McGhee resigned from the party and became the state's first prominent African-American Democrat in the city and in 1896 was chosen as the first African-American delegate to a Democratic National Convention, which that year was held in Kansas City, Kansas. In 1898, along with eleven others, he helped to found the American Law Enforcement League, who published their Manifesto to, "abolish Jim Crow railroad cars, make lynching a crime, and to enforce the 14th and 15th Amendments." He continued his activism in the struggle for civil rights in 1901 when he visited several cities, at his own expense, to raise money to test the constitutionality of Louisiana's laws to deprive African-Americans of their right to vote.

Another group interested in African-American rights was the Minnesota Chapter of the National Association of Colored Women, which was organized in 1902.

The organization took place at 782 Selby Avenue, which was the home of Mrs. T.H. Lyles, who was elected their president. Laura Hickman was elected secretary and Mrs. A. Johnson, of Duluth, as corresponding secretary. The group later became known as the Minnesota State Association of Colored Women.

Mrs. T.H. Lyles

32

CHAPTER FOUR 1900 – 1919

In the fall of 1903, Charles E. James, the African-American leader of the Leather Boot Workers, was elected President of the St. Paul Trades and Labor Assembly for two successive six-month terms.

In 1905, after W.E.B. DuBois spoke at St. James A.M.E. Church, McGhee's wife, Mattie, gave a reception for him at their home at 665 University Avenue. McGhee's contributions to the organization of the NAACP began later that summer in Ontario, Canada, where Dubois was forced to meet after being unable to acquire accommodations in Buffalo, New York. Dubois had invited McGhee and 28 other delegates to map out a structure for a new civil rights group. Dubois was elected General Secretary and George H. Jackson was chosen General Treasurer. The group's first objectives were to demand compulsory school attendance for all children and to end the vicious practice of using African-Americans as strike-breakers. They also demanded an end to discrimination in unions and benefits for African-American war veterans.

In 1906, in a letter to President Theodore Roosevelt, McGhee vigorously protested some of the reasons why he considered Roosevelt's treatment of the 1st Battalion of the 25th Infantry Battalion highly prejudicial.

He mentioned that some of these Brownsville, Texas soldiers had been formerly stationed at Fort Snelling and decried the fact that they had been given dishonorable discharges based on purely circumstantial evidence and that despite the absence of either confessions or informants, he had accepted the worst about these soldiers and the hastily drawn recommendations of his Inspector General Ernest A. Garlington. The consequences of which resulted in 167 men, six of whom were Congressional Medal of Honor recipients, being barred for life from their pensions, all further military service and any civilian employment with the federal government. McGhee also reminded Roosevelt that four years earlier, he had publicly declared, "I know the bravery and character of the 25th Infantry soldiers. They saved my life at El Caney and I have had occasion to say so in many articles and speeches. The

Rough Riders were in a bad way when they were rescued by the 9th and 10th Calvary, who rushed to our aid carrying everything before them. The African-American soldier has the facility of coming to the front when he is most needed!"[1]

With the 1906 Congressional elections coming up, Roosevelt deliberately delayed his decision to reprimand the men until November 7th, the day after the elections, to ensure that Republicans would retain control of the House and prevent a possible slump in the African-American Republican vote.

W.E.B. Dubois

Dubois gave credit for the founding of the Niagara Movement to McGhee. After its second meeting at Harper's Ferry, the movement lost some of its momentum, but in 1907, the rally drew a crowd of over eight hundred, who heard Dubois condemn Roosevelt for his betrayal of the African-American regiment who had made him famous.

Dubois was rewarded the following year, when a race riot in Springfield, Ohio, so disturbed Mary White Ovington that she called together a small biracial group in New York City under the leadership of Oswald Garrison Villard to discuss it. Out of this meeting came the formation of the National Committee for the Advancement of the Negro Race, which in 1909 evolved into the National Association for the Advancement of Colored People. It was founded on the one hundredth anniversary of Lincoln's birthday.

At a dinner, in Newport, given in his honor, in May 1911, McGhee ended his remarks with these comments, "I have lived to help my race and in trying to help them, I will die. I need no monument. I hope I have built in your hearts and memories a monument more lasting than any of stone or bronze. To have you tell your children, even as you have told me tonight that my life was worth living and my days have been well spent within the service of others means much to me. If I pass, you need not bring any flowers. The flowers I want as I lay on death's bed are these words, 'That I served well of my fellowmen.'" The following April, McGhee and Dr. Valdo Turner were chosen by the newly formed Twin Cities Protective League to represent them at the NAACP convention in Chicago. Upon his return, McGhee and his wife, Mattie, left for their cabin on Apple River near Amery, Wisconsin. They had among their guests, Dr. Daniel Hale Williams, the African-American surgeon who had been the first doctor in America to perform successful surgery on the human heart. There was also a Mr. Julius Avendorph and Dr. W.E. Watkins. The group spent two weeks fishing with their catch ranging in size from five to twelve pounds.

Just prior to their return to St. Paul, McGhee bruised his right leg while attempting to catch a turkey. It appeared to be slight but he had ruptured a blood vessel, which formed a clot. Over the weekend he was told to use crutches for two weeks. Unfortunately, the thrombosis progressed to his lung which caused him to contract pneumonia and by September 19th little hope was given for a recovery. He died only six weeks shy of his 51st birthday. His funeral was held on September 23rd at St. Peter Claver where Father Stephen Theobald

Frederick McGhee

noted, "There was not a time when Fred McGhee, as a citizen, ever allied himself to any political party or espoused any of its principles when he allowed himself to ever forget what he had most at heart, the interests of his own people. These he stood by with all the devotion and grit of a man of action and a man of power and when party principles and the interest of his race clashed, his race always claimed his allegiance. Such is the public man who will live long in the hearts of the people he served. Like all public men he had enemies, which is unavoidable in public life; but what is that, compared to friends? The host of loyal friends he had could always be summoned to his side. I have seen, during my short time in St. Paul, how Fred McGhee has stood almost alone for the rights of his people. Many a time he fought and lost but when he faced defeat he always lost gamely." McGhee, was survived by his wife Mattie and his 22-year old adopted daughter, Ruth, and was laid to rest from St. Peter Claver Church in Calvary Cemetery although another memorial service was given on the 29th at Pilgrim Baptist Church where a eulogy was given by Mayor C. D. O'Brien. While in New York, W.E.B. DuBois eulogized him as, "a champion of the colored race" in the Crisis.

The person who continued his advocacy role in the community was his Republican friend, William Trevane Francis. Francis, had been born in Indianapolis, Indiana, on April 26, 1869 where he was to receive his elementary and secondary education. He arrived in St. Paul in 1888 and went on to receive his L.L.B. degree from the St. Paul College of Law in 1904. After his graduation, he served as a legal clerk for the Northern Pacific Railway Company for the next six years and in 1911 he was promoted to chief clerk of its legal department. After McGhee's death, Francis was invited by Mrs. McGhee to take over his offices on the Union Block at Fourth and Cedar as well as his very active practice. Another part of McGhee's advocacy role was also taken over by Francis when he was asked to chair the leadership of the Twin City Protective League that McGhee had helped to found.

In 1913, the Protective League was represented at the national NAACP convention by Dr. Valdo Turner. His wife also accompanied him and was cited during the convention for her efforts in raising a thousand dollars to help keep the Crisis magazine solvent. The previous summer she had organized a "Festival of Race Music" at Bowlby Hall on Sixth and Robert Streets and engaged the service of the popular McCullough Orchestra. In September on the anniversary of McGhee's death, an organizational meeting was called for October 6th. At that meeting, 17 members of the Twin City Branch formed their own St. Paul branch with the Reverend A.M. Lealtad as their president. Founding members included Dr. and Mrs. Valdo Turner, Mrs. T.H. Lyles, Jose Sherwood, W.T. Francis, J.H. Loomis, O.C. Hall and J.Q. Adams.

The St. Paul Branch began planning immediately for a Lincoln memorial meeting the following month at the Plymouth Congregational Church with a program that included Governor Adolph O. Eberhart and the President of both the University of Minnesota and Macalester College.

By 1913, Adams had fallen on bad times. The chain of newspapers he had once headed had been drastically reduced. The *Appeal* offices in Dallas, Washington D.C., St. Louis and Louisville had all been closed and he had been forced to sell the Chicago *Appeal* to his brother. However, his pithy editorials continued to point out the myths, anomalies and ironies of America's racial policies as well as to chastise his readers, on occasion, for their refusal to unite and support causes that he felt would ameliorate their condition. That June, he had noted that Patrick Ford, of New York, had raised five thousand dollars for the Irish National Fund and chided his readers, "How much have we raised for our national NAACP?" He also reminded his readers that the U.S. Supreme Court had declared the anti-discrimination clauses of the Civil Rights Act of 1875 as null and void on the grounds that it was not applicable uniformly throughout the country and was thus unconstitutional…" He noted, wryly, that since the nation's highest tribunal had only once decided anything in favor of the ten million African-Americans in the country, its action were not in the least surprising. That summer, he re-printed an essay by Maggie Walker of the *St. Luke Herald*, of Richmond, Virginia.

THE POWER OF AGITATION

The greatest power on earth for the righting of wrongs is the power of agitation. When the spirit and power of agitation dies among a people, they are doomed beyond all hope of resuscitation and redemption. So important is the power that it is guaranteed to the people through the Constitution. That the colored man should not be an agitator has been dinned into his ears until it reached his very soul.

He has been constantly told that all he has to do toward righting his wrongs is to wait until the Lord, Himself, shall see fit to come down and right them. Often, when he starts an agitation and is rebuffed at the start, he loses heart and abandons the effort and gives up like a disappointed child. It is the agitation of the waters of the sea which prevents its stagnation and death. It is the agitation of the air which gives us pure air to breathe. It is the agitation of our blood which gives us breath, the power of motion and life and it is the agitation of our brain which gives us ideas and saves us from mental torpor. When People lose their desire for agitation and quietly submit to wrongs, they court death and eventual genocide.[2]

In February 1914, W.T. Francis took on the case of Pullman Porter George T. Williams, who had been arrested earlier that month on the word of his supervisor, who had accused him of being drunk and disorderly after he had arrived late to work. Williams vehemently contended that he was neither drunk nor disorderly and that when he attempted to explain his reasons for his tardiness, his supervisors simply refused to listen and instead called the police and had him locked up. Francis was not only able to have the charges dropped, but he won Williams an award of $2,999.99 for "malicious prosecution." It was the largest amount ever awarded a plaintiff in a Ramsey County civil suit up to that time.[3]

In the spring of that year, O.C. Hall, a former proprietor of one of St. Paul's finest African-American barbershops and at this time a clerk in the

City-Auditor's office, became a champion for African-American workers in the public works department. In a letter to the editor of the *St. Paul Pioneer Press*, he protested the discharge of local African-American workers on the asphalt crews and the hiring of strike-breakers, who had been brought in from Indianapolis to work at lower wages. As a result of his agitation, a meeting was held and an African-American labor organization was formed with G. T. Williams as its president, O.C. Hall as its secretary and R.M. Johnson as its treasurer. They succeeded in enrolling 26 members and were successful in recovering the lost public works jobs. They were represented in their negotiations by attorney J. Louis Ervin.[4]

That summer, in a July editorial, Adams denounced the African-American men who had watched the lynching of Rosa Carson, an African-American woman in Orangeburg, South Carolina. He declared it was, "a disgrace that 30 Afro-American males would fail to give their lives in an attempt to prevent the lynching of one of their women. They could not have died in a holier cause and it would have made the next mob hesitate as all mobs are cowardly. Any Afro-American man who would stand by and see the law outraged and one of their women lynched is worse than a coward."[5]

Also that summer, the St. Paul Branch of the NAACP selected Father Stephen Theobald to represent them at the NAACP national convention in Baltimore. While at the NAACP conference's opening session, Theobald presented a paper on "The Catholic Church and the Negro." The national body had grown to 50 branches and almost 7000 members with the St. Paul branch having just over 100.

Theobald had been born in Georgetown, Demerrara, British Guiana, South America, on July 5, 1874 and during his early years had been educated by the Jesuits at St. Stanislaus

Father Stephen Theobald

Academy before being accepted at Queens College, in England, which prepared him to enter Cambridge where he earned his L.L.D. degree from that institution in 1905 before migrating to Canada. There, he worked for 16 months on the editorial staff of the Montreal Daily Star. After making written inquires to Archbishop Ireland about the priesthood, he received an invitation to enter the St. Paul Seminary after completing some preliminary tests which had been sent. Ireland had been amazed by the erudition of Theobald's responses.

Theobald entered the Seminary in the fall of 1905 and achieved a brilliant record before his ordination by Bishop Patrick Heffron, on Winona, on June 6, 1910. He said his first Mass on June 12th and was assigned to the Archdiocese as Ireland's Canon Lawyer, but also gave assistance to Father Printon at St. Peter Claver which was then located on Aurora and Farington Streets. While there, Theobald raised money to install three white marble columns in the sanctuary and a large mural over the altar, which depicted Saint Peter Claver in his Columbian apostolate.

In the spring of 1915, Dr. Valdo Turner, along with other members of the St. Paul branch of the NAACP, protested to Mayor Powers and the Garrick Theatre's plan to show a movie entitled, "The Nigger." The manager of the theatre was called in by the Mayor and after considerable negotiations he agreed to allow Mrs. T.H. Lyles' committee to preview the film and some of the more objectionable scenes were cut and the film was re-titled, "The New Governor." [6]

In October, J.Q. Adams, in a fiery editorial condemned a rally of some of New York's "Greatest Leaders" for congratulating the country because in 1913, only 52 blacks had been lynched, shot or burned by mobs that year. Adams declared, "If that can give any satisfaction to ten million blacks, what in God's name will make them fight? … As for me, as long as one black man is illegally punished or unjustly treated or has the door of opportunity closed in his face, I will protest and protest again…"[7]

By November, the number of African-Americans lynched in the country increased to almost one hundred, due in large part to the showing of "The Birth of a Nation" which was based on the life of Confederate General Bedford Forest, the commander of the Fort Pillow Massacre, and who had subsequently served as the Ku Klux Klan's first Imperial Wizard. That same month, W.T. Francis submitted his proposed ordinance to ban hate films. The City Council simply laid it over, but he did succeed in getting them to issue an injunction against the showing of the D.W. Griffith film and Adams commented editorially, "We hope the Twin Cities has seen the last of that production forever!"[8]

The following January, Francis spoke on the race problem to a group at the German Methodist Church in St. Paul. He noted in his remarks that St. Paul now had an African-American population of over 5000 citizens who owned $51,000 worth of fraternal property and had only a 3.4 percent illiteracy rate. He also noted that according to the 1910 Census, African-Americans in the nation had 27 published authors, 17,495 homes and operated 20 million acres of farmland worth more than one billion dollars. He also told his audience that the "Negro" problem in this country was mainly due to the actions of persons like Senators Vardaman and Tillman and authors like Thomas Dixon, who had fanned the flames of hate and created the political and social climate that denied equal rights to African-Americans.[9]

Francis also gave credit to Minnesota's Senator Moses E. Clapp who he noted was one of the few U.S. Senators who could be relied upon to support measures of interest to African-American voters. In June, the NAACP called upon its members to write Senator Clapp that summer to protest the prohibition of intermarriage in the nation's capitol as well as the continued use of Jim Crow street cars which he declared were both un-Christian and a disgrace to show world visitors.[10]

In the Spring of 1917, Francis became the first local African-American to run for the 38th District South seat in the legislature though after winning the primary, he lost in the general election, while

Attorney J. Louis Ervin became the first African-American attorney to win an acquittal for an African-American defendant in St. Paul. His client, Wesley Gresham had been accused of killing a white saloon proprietor in a one-sided and unfair brawl.

Meanwhile, in a subsequent editorial Adams grumbled that even though the army needed an additional 40,000 men to fill their "colored" quota they still required them to await the draft and refused their attempts to enlist.[11]

In September, Francis was again an advocate when Grace Lealtad, the daughter of the pastor of St. Phillips Episcopal Church, was denied her teaching assignment at Hill Elementary School because of protests from white parents. Francis headed the NAACP legal committee who confronted Commissioner of Education Wunderlich and demanded that she be given back her assignment. Wunderlich refused to concede and affirmed her re-assignment to Crowley School to teach slow learners. After repeated protests from the NAACP as well as her parents, she was finally allowed to teach at Jackson Elementary School.[12]

In January 1918, Mrs. Ethel Howard Maxwell, the President of the Minnesota Federation of Colored Women, protested to the *St. Paul Pioneer Press* about their editorial which suggested that the city's "pickaninnies" should have a separate weigh-in center at the Welcome Hall Community House rather than being weighed in with white children at Jackson Elementary School's Weigh-In-Center. After a number of phone calls, Mrs. Maxwell finally received an apology from the paper's editor and a call from Mrs. J.T. Hale who told her that the Ramsey County Women's War Organization had decided to support the weigh-ins at Jackson Elementary, and it would now be open for all babies.[13]

Ethel Howard Maxwell

The following month, as a result of the riots that had occurred in Houston, Texas, the *Appeal's* pages were filled with accounts of the fighting that started after a African-American woman had been brutally treated by a white police officer. Fifty-nine men from the 24th Regiment were convicted of various offenses as a result of those riots and twenty-nine sentenced to death while the others received long terms of imprisonment. Just three days before Christmas, 13 of the 29 men were hung. Of the remaining doomed 16, President Wilson commuted the sentences of six but the remaining ten were later hung.[14]

After the riots, many soldiers, as well as large segments of the public, protested to the Boston Guardian about the abuse of the word Negro in the Houston affair which caused publisher William M. Trotter to announce that henceforth his paper would use the term "colored" rather than "Negro" to designate African-Americans and his efforts helped to popularized the term in future decades.

In an address in March 1918, W.T. Francis reminded his audience, at St. Paul's Main Library, that the YMCA on Tenth and Cedar was still rejecting African-American memberships and that the Wilder Baths on Seven Corners was still ignoring their donor's wish that the baths be used by all "the worthy poor of St. Paul regardless of race."[15]

Also that spring, Adams told his subscribers that after both houses of the Puerto Rican Legislature had voted to end segregation in their armed forces, their bill was vetoed by President Wilson who ordered their troops re-segregated.[16]

In an address given in May to the local YMCA, Francis boasted of the gains made by the city's African-American community. He noted that there were now 600 Baptist, 550 Methodist, 250 Catholic, 200 Episcopalian and 175 Presbyterian. There were nineteen fraternal organizations, two of which were the Odd Fellows and the Masons who owned Union Hall on the northwest corner of Aurora and Kent Streets. The community also had three lawyers, two doctors, two dentists, one architectural draftsman, one public school teacher, one electrical engineer, and one civil engineer who was also the foreman of a street paving crew.

In the semi-professional area the community had one real estate agency, one publicist with the Northern Pacific Railroad, a bookkeeper at Finch, Young and McCoonville Wholesale Dry Goods Company, a candy-maker at Maud Borup's Shop and a clerk in the County Auditor's office.

In the business field, the community had twenty-seven barbershops, five pool halls, seven restaurants, one picture framing store, (Lowe's Art and Picture Framing Shoppe), one masseuse, one grocery store, one millinery shop, one Ladies Turkish Bath, one piano-polisher and one phonograph repairman.

Finally in the civil service area there was one policeman, three detectives, one railway mail clerk, seven mail carriers, eleven postal clerks and twelve firemen.[17]

That summer, the *Appeal* carried a copy of a letter, which Adams had sent to the National NAACP with five dollars, "to start a fund to fight all Jim Crow army legislation brought up before the Congress". Between June 5, 1917, and November 11, 1918, of the 3,350 African-American men in Minnesota who had registered with the Selective Service, only 511 were actually inducted.

African-American commissioned officers from St. Paul included 1st Lieutenant Sam Ransom, Captain J.R. French, who was later demoted to 1st Lieutenant after induction into the U.S. Dental Corps, 2nd Lieutenant Paul Wigington and 2nd Lieutenant Hugh Schuck of the 367th Infantry Regiment. That September, William Godette became the first African-American Minnesota recruit to receive a battlefield commission from the Army.[18]

That fall, the Secretary of War announced that there were no prospects for the enrollment of any more African-American medical officers in the army as their quota had been reached. African-American physicians were thus left with the prospect of being inducted into the service as privates under the new draft law.[19]

Despite the rampant racism and discrimination in the country's armed services, 42,000 African-American troops did service in combat units which was about 11 percent of the 380,000 African-American in the wartime army. The vast majority of the combat soldiers served in the 92nd and 93rd Divisions and others manned four under-strength groups with the 9th and 10th Calvary Regiments and the 24th and 25th Infantry Regiments.

The bill introduced into the Minnesota Legislature for a Colored unit in the Minnesota National Guard was defeated and the response of the African-American community, in St. Paul, was to form their own Minnesota Home Guard, under the command of Major Jose Sherwood and Captain Clarence W. Wigington. A Company had Earl Weber as its 1st Lieutenant and J. Homer Goins as its 2nd Lieutenant. Company B had Orrington C. Hall as its 1st Lieutenant and T.W. Stepp as its 2nd in command.[20]

In December, on the eve of President Wilson's departure for the Peace Table in France, editor Adams, in an Open letter to him, pleaded on the pages of the *Appeal* for home rule for all the world's colonies that desire it, self-determination for all races of color, the abrogation of the white-only policy in Australia and an end to America's Oriental Exclusion Act of 1917. He also pleaded for a new naturalization law for Africans, the Japanese, Chinese and the Malayans as well as citizenship for the American Indians. Finally, he asked for a color-blind clause in the Charter of the League, eliminating all color restrictions on immigration between countries.[21]

On February 20, 1919, the Pan-African Congress opened in Paris, with ten representatives from the United States led by William Monroe Trotter who represented the National Equal Rights League and had come to the Paris conference despite the U.S. State Department's refusal to grant him a passport. Upon his arrival he worked long hours petitioning representatives to the conference to pass his N.E.R.L. resolutions and informing his French hosts of the discriminatory practices of the American army toward its African-American soldiers as well as examples of brutality towards African-American citizens throughout the U.S.[22]

With the advent of the war, the flow of immigrants from Europe had dropped from 1.2 million in 1914 to 110,618 in 1918. To meet these new labor demands, an estimated 300,000 to 1,000,000 African-American people had left the South in the Great Migration between 1910 and 1920. Many came as a result of the urging of Robert Abbot, the publisher of the *Chicago Defender*, who used Pullman porters and entertainers to spread his gospel of "Exodus from the South."

His editorials often pointed out that farm workers in the South were averaging only 50 cents a day while domestics made only $1.50 a day and noted that factory laborers in the North were receiving two to three times that much. His anti-lynching motto was, "If you must die, take at least one with you!" and his paper described countless examples of widespread peonage, poor schools and most of all, that in the North, African-Americans were more likely to be treated as men and women rather than as children. The feeling was best described in a letter written by a African-American preacher to a friend back home.

"Well, we're treated more like men up here in the North. That's the secret of it. There's prejudice here too, but the color line isn't drawn in our faces at every turn as it is in the South. It all gets back to the question of manhood!"[23]

From 1915–1920, many who left the South were the educated and professional people whom DuBois had chosen to call the "Talented

Tenth." Though many were persuaded to come North, the exodus had only a mild effect on Minnesotans. In St. Paul, the population increase had only been about 7.3 percent or from 3,144 to 3,376 and the State's overall African-American population growth only went from 7,084 to 8,809.[24]

On the eve of the new decade, over half of St. Paul's African-Americans had been born in the South. Many of the newly arrived found work on the many railroads that bisected the city or the meat-packing plants in South St. Paul.

Other African-American immigrants found work in a variety of personal service or unskilled labor jobs while many of the women found work as domestics. A few of the migrants, during this period, were stone-masons who helped complete the building of the State Capitol.

The flow of southern African-American migrants sometimes generated feeling of hostility among the majority community purely from racial prejudice. Some animosity also occurred among members of the northern African-American community members who sometimes disparaged the newcomers' "down home ways." The area where many of these newcomers tended to live was on Rondo between Dale and Rice Streets which was often referred to by some as "Cornmeal Valley," but Earl Wilkins, editor of the Echo, found it a wonderful street which was, "a riot of warm colors, feelings and sounds, with sights that would make one from the rural South feel at home and a person from Harlem or State Street, at ease. Music is in abundance from Victrolas, saxophones, player pianos and hurry-up orchestras which pour out their complaints to the passing scene. It seethes with the pulsating beauty of the lives of its people who feel intensely every emotion which stirs their beings…"

Before the 1918 legislature recessed, they passed a Housing Bill (H.R. 507:18), which outlawed restrictive covenants based on religious beliefs. Shortly before its passage, George Karom, an African-American citizen, won a judgment of $1,500 from a white real estate agent named J.

McLaughlin who had promised him four choice lots near the corner of Dale and Wheelock Parkway, but had switched the deeds at the last minute to four lots located on sandy soil on Rondo near Oxford.[25]

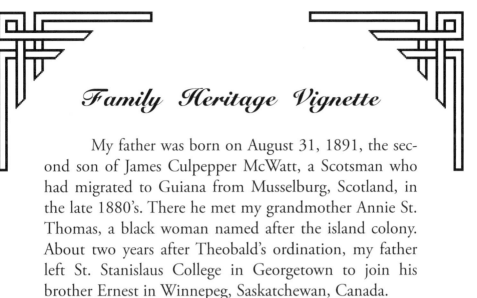

Family Heritage Vignette

My father was born on August 31, 1891, the second son of James Culpepper McWatt, a Scotsman who had migrated to Guiana from Musselburg, Scotland, in the late 1880's. There he met my grandmother Annie St. Thomas, a black woman named after the island colony. About two years after Theobald's ordination, my father left St. Stanislaus College in Georgetown to join his brother Ernest in Winnepeg, Saskatchewan, Canada.

After a son, Ernest, was born my father, Arthur Clarendon, followed and later the couple had two daughters, Florrie and Maggie. After working his way over to Canada aboard a freighter, my father was rebuffed by Ernest who had arrived earlier and had married a Canadian woman and was left to fend for himself in the strange new land. Dad eventually managed to obtain work as a dining car waiter on the Canadian Pacific and had himself smuggled across the Minnesota border in a linen closet. After his arrival, in St. Paul, he was offered lodgings by Sidney Salter, a waiter, who helped him find work on the Northern Pacific Railroad. Salters later introduced him to my mother, Carrie Lowe, whom he wed on October 27th, 1915.

CHAPTER FOUR BIBLIOGRAPHY

1. *Appeal*, 20 September 1906.

2. *Appeal*, 17 October 1914.

3. *Appeal*, 14 February 1914.

4. Arthur C. McWatt, "St. Paul's Resourceful African-American Community", *Ramsey County History*, Spring, 1991, p. 7.

5. *Appeal*, 18 July 1914.

6. *Appeal*, 10 April 1915.

7. *Appeal*, 10 October 1915.

8. *Appeal*, 6 November 1915.

9. *Appeal*, 15 January 1916.

   That year President Wilson further fanned the flames of white supremacy by inviting D.W. Griffith to show his film, "The Birth of a Nation", at the White House, The Civil War in American Memory, by David Blight, Harvard University Press, Cambridge, Mass., 2001.

10. *Appeal*, 10 June 1916

11. *Appeal*, 7 July 1917.

12. *Appeal*, 3 September 1917.

13. *Appeal*, 6 January 1918.

14. *Appeal*, 23 February 1918.

15. *Appeal*, 22 March 1918.

16. *Appeal*, 30 March 1918.

17. *Appeal*, 8 May 1918.

18. *Appeal*, 7 September 1918.

19. Spangler, *The Negro in Minnesota*, p. 90.

20. *Appeal*, 21 September 1918.

21. Spangler, ibid..

22. Fox Steven R., *William Monroe Trotter; The Guardian of Boston*, Anthenum Press, New York, 1970, p. 227.

23. Baker, Ray Stannard, *Following the Color Line*, Harpers Ros, New York City, NY, 1964, p. 133.

24. Spangler, *The Negro in Minnesota*, p. 96.

25. *Appeal*, 7 December 1918.

Chapter Five
1920 – 1929

"When a people lose their desire for agitation and begin to quietly submit to wrong and oppression they are courting mental suicide and race genocide."

Maggie Walker, Editor, St. Luke Herald, Appeal 10/17/14

In 1920, a commission of the Federal Council of Churches conducted a survey of what Negroes in America wanted and after analyzing the results they concluded that their primary concerns were for universal suffrage, better educational facilities, the abolition of segregation, equality in the military, equal wages and better housing and sanitation facilities. When the Nineteenth Amendment was passed on August 1920, the Council concluded that at least the first segments of those needs were fulfilled. Monroe Trotter responded to their conclusion by sending an open letter to Mrs. Carrie C. Catt, which Adams printed in his *Appeal*. His letter suggested that the first American Women's Suffrage Convention grew out of an anti-slavery convention and though Lucretia Coffin Mott was denied an opportunity to vote, the champion who rose and sustained the movement at its darkest hour was Frederick Douglass. Trotter also called upon the followers of both Cady Stanton and Susan B. Anthony, "to vow in their hour of victory that political freedom should not continue to ignore race discrimination."

At the Republican convention in Minneapolis that year, attorney Francis, was elected a Presidential Elector, while his friend, Valdo Turner, was elected board chairman of the St. Paul Branch of the NAACP. Both of them had worked hard in forming the branch and, recently, to prevent an anti-miscegenation bill from becoming law in the Minnesota legislature. Dr. Turner was on the staff of St. John's Hospital and had testified against the bill which would have defined African-Americans as those having one-eighth amount of African blood and would have made interracial marriages a misdemeanor and would not recognize those which had been performed outside of the state.

In January 1920, Dr. Turner protested vigorously to the *St. Paul Pioneer Press* in its designation of the Welcome Hall Playground, on the northeast corner of Western and Rondo, as being, "exclusively for our colored." Editor Adams echoed his sentiments by also decrying the paper's continual use of the epithets, dago, Dutchy, froggy, greaser, heiny, howat, hunky, kike, mick, paddy, sheeny and wop and suggested they also eliminate the use of nigger, darky, coon, shine, smoke, dingy and picaninny to their list.[1]

The country was trying to recover from the previous year's "Red Summer" when 25 bloody race riots had occurred throughout the nation.

On June 14th, the St. Paul NAACP was called to face one of its greatest challenges when it was informed of the arrest of six young black men who worked for a carnival, which had been playing in Duluth. They had been charged with an alleged assault of a 19 year-old white girl and were being held in the city jail.

The following night a mob, which some say numbered between five and ten thousand persons, stormed the jail and seized Isaac McGhee, Elmer Jackson and Elias Clayton from their cells and took them out and lynched them from a light pole on First Street and left their bodies hanging in full view of the public. McGhee had not even been a suspect and had been jailed only as a potential witness.[2] When the rope had been placed around his neck, a priest, the Reverend William J. Powers, fought his way forward and climbed several feet up the pole and yelled, "Men, you don't know if this man is guilty. I ask you, in the name of God, to stop!" A man, in the mob yelled back, "This has nothing to do with God!" McGhee was hoisted up where he convulsed and died within minutes.[3]

Both Twin City branches of the NAACP raised funds for the impending trial and Governor J.A. Burnquist, the president of the St. Paul NAACP, reported Attorney J. Louis Ervin's findings to the local and national offices. A NAACP office was set-up in Duluth with F.L. Barnett in charge.[4]

At the inquiry, Dr. David Graham, who had examined the girl the night of the alleged assault, made no mention of a gonorrhea infection that she had and reported, "that evidence of an assault was inconclusive" and, told the jury, "I cannot say for sure whether or not she was raped."[5]

Despite his hesitancy, 28 charges were brought against 14 suspects who were jailed. By November, Judge Cant had dismissed charges against 12 of them. Only William Miller and Max Mason were tried and Attorney Charles Scrutchin was successful in getting Miller acquitted. During Mason's trial, a Dr. Nicholson examined him and declared that he had gonorrhea, despite Mason's denial. A Dr. Coventry examined the female plaintiff who had earlier testified that she was infected. The fact that she had told the court that she noticed the infection three days before the alleged assault and Dr. Coventry's testimony that the infection would only appear one to ten days after sexual contact did not appear to effect the subsequent decisions of the jurors. Mason was denied his request to have a second doctor's opinion as to whether he was infected and was found guilty on November 27th and remanded to Stillwater Prison where he served the next four years.[6]

Only two of the eighteen members of the lynch mob were found guilty of instigating a riot and both served nominal sentences.

In 1921, Nellie Griswold Francis' successful lobbying efforts resulted in the passage of an anti-lynching law in the Minnesota Legislature which was sponsored by Representatives George Nordlin, Theodore Christenson and J. Leven and its passage effectively ended that type of atrocity in Minnesota. It was likely due to the $7,500 fine it imposed on perpetrators and the dire consequences it promised law officers who permitted them.

After the ratification of the Nineteenth Amendment that fall, the newly organized League of Women Voters invited Francis to serve as hostess to their installation dinner at the Curtis Hotel.[7]

The following April, the League welcomed Mesdames J.W. Blair, J.C. Black, G.A. Gooden, A.J. Foster, W.R. Hardy and M. Green to their meeting at the University Club on Summit Avenue.[8]

In June, Adams wrote a letter to the Secretary of War, John W. Weeks, to object to the use of African-American troops only in the 92nd and 93rd Infantry Regiments and not in their state guard units. He argued that it was not only un-democratic, but it denied them the right of full citizenship and placed on them, "the badge of a pariah caste." The following week, Secretary Weeks sent Adams his reply and told him that his objections were the first he had ever received.[9]

Also that month, Minneapolitan Lena O. Smith, who graduated from Northwestern College of Law, became the state's first African-American woman to pass a state bar exam.[10]

In October, attorney Gale Hilyard appeared before Governor James A. O. Preus on behalf of the St. Paul NAACP to plead a stay of extradition of an African-American fugitive, Andrew Jackson Smitherman, who had been arrested after fleeing the Tulsa-Greenwood Massacre. The race riot had burned and looted 34 square blocks of the African-American district and resulted in the death of approximately 185 African-American men, women and children as well as the destruction of 1,200 buildings including the "Negro Wall Street of America." The Governor denied the group's petition; however, the branch decided to send clothing to the African-American victims of the riot.[11]

Later that month, Adams noted that though the Dyer Anti-Lynching Bill had passed the House by a 230–119 majority, it had been later filibustered by southern Senators and then abandoned by the Republican leadership who betrayed their African-American constituents.

As the Christmas season approached, the Hall Brothers Barber Shop in the Pittsburgh Building wrote Adams to ask if he would tell his readers to let them know of any jobs available for African-American men as they were interested in finding work for them and were charging no fees.[12]

In the spring of 1922, African-American Attorney Evan Anderson filed for State Representative for the 38th District, though he subsequently lost the election to John J. McDonough.

Meanwhile, Adams continued to remind his readers that since the introduction of the Dyer Anti-Lynching Bill in the House, on April 11th, 38 persons had been murdered by mobs in the U.S., with two victims having been burned alive and four burned after their hangings. One victim was an African-American man who had merely asked a white woman why she had not replied to a note he had written her.[13]

That summer, W.T. Francis was appointed to the Advisory Board of the Federal Employees League and reported to Adams that he was somewhat surprised to discover, while in the Capitol City, that Harding appointee Perry W. Howard was a not a Special Assistant Attorney General as had been reported to the African-American press but was instead a special assistant to the U.S. Attorney General and also that Emmet J. Scott was not an Assistant Secretary of War to Secretary Baker and did not make an annual salary of $5,000 as had been reported, but was instead merely a confidential clerk to the Secretary at the much lower annual salary of $1,200.

That year also marked the passing of one of our state's major civil rights contributors, J. Francis Wheaton. Wheaton died in New York from asphyxiation at the age of 55. His death appeared to be a suicide as he had been despondent over the need to pay a $5,000 dollar bail bond, which he had co-signed for a former friend. Credited with having led the fight to amend the state's major civil rights bill at the turn of the century, he was survived by his second wife, Dora, whom he married in 1916. Over 50,000 people lined the streets of Harlem to observe his funeral cortege which included 5,000 Elks.

In September, the African-American community of St. Paul was energized by the formation of the St. Paul Business League, who held an exhibition at Union Hall. Thirty booths were set up displaying over 50 different products manufactured by local entrepreneurs.

In January 1923, Dr. Turner and the NAACP protested the unfair treatment accorded the city's packing-house workers. During the protests, Frank Hardy and Nick Bowens were arrested by the police and were charged with assault for resisting arrest.

In the spring, Charles Sumner Smith, brought charges against the Minnesota Boxing Commission, of which he was a member. He charged them with violating the Fourteenth Amendment to the U.S. Constitution by enacting a rule, which forbade mixed boxing matches in the state. He was successful in having an injunction served on the commission until the rule was abrogated. It resulted in the staging of the state's first mixed bout, which took place in St. Paul.

In May, W.T. Francis was successful in bringing Thomas Arnold of the National Urban League to St. Paul for ten days to discuss the organization of the Twin-City branch. Arnold brought $500 with him from the national office and was able to combine it with $575 that Ed Hall and Roy Wilkins had raised from a dance. The St. Paul Community Chest was so impressed by their organizing efforts that they promised to take over most of their funding that fall. The first board meeting was held on May 7th and S. Ed Hall was elected their chairman with George McLeod the first president, W. T. Francis vice-president, Roy Wilkins secretary and Norman Mears treasurer. Other founding members included Henry High, Charles Weschcke, E.H. Miller, T.R. Morgan, Owen Howell, Dr. Earl Weber, Dr. Valdo D. Turner and Fred

McCracken. Elmer Carter, a Harvard graduate, who had been working with the Louisville branch, was persuaded to take the job of Executive Director and began work on August 1st.[14]

The primary tasks of the Twin City branch were outlined in its charter which said, in part, it was, "to try and bring about more cooperation among existing community agencies, to try and improve social and economic conditions within the colored communities and to assist in activities to improve relations between the white and colored peoples of both cities." Operations began on September 17th in offices located in the McClure Building, at 61 East Sixth Street and their first allocation for the 1923–24 budget was for $4,881.16 and came in November.[15]

J.Q. Adams in an editorial had lamented the poor relations between the communities with the burning of a fiery cross on Bass Lake, which was seven miles northwest of the Twin Cities. Charles Chapman owned the property, a local African-American man. Over 100 masked and robed followers led a procession of 500 persons in a rally in a hollow close to Chapman's cabin.[16]

That month, the local African-American community was saddened to hear that the second pillar of their civil rights triumvirate, J.Q. Adams had been struck and killed while attempting to board a street car at University and Fry Streets. He died the following day and his funeral was attended by hundreds of St. Paulites and out-of-town friends. Adams was truly the quintessence of the Protest Tradition and served as an agitator or advocate as the situation demanded, but his real strength was in his spiritual activism which helped carry civil rights protest into the modern age. His funeral was held at Pilgrim Baptist Church and was conducted by the Elks Lodge.

The *Appeal* Publishing Company was re-organized with John Q. Adams Jr. as its president with his wife, Adina Gibbs Adams as vice president, Roy Wilkins as treasurer and Odell D. Smith as secretary.

In October, the St. Paul Equal Rights League sent a petition to the recently sworn-in President Calvin Coolidge to ask his support for the Dyer Bill, the acceptance of African-American cadets at West Point and Annapolis, a pardon for the 24th Infantry prisoners and the abolition of segregation and discrimination in the Civil Service and in the nation's capitol. The League had attorney Hammond Turner as its president, W.R. Hardy as its vice-president and J.W. Walton as its treasurer.[17]

Later that month, Joshia Trice, an African-American tackle for the University of Minnesota football team wrote in his diary, on the eve of an important game, "The honor of my race, family and self are at stake. "Everyone is expecting me to do big things. I will! My whole body and soul are to be thrown recklessly about on the field tomorrow. Beware of the mass interference, fight low with your eyes open and toward the play. Roll back the interference. Watch out for the crossbuck and reverse runs. Be on your toes every minute as I am expected to be especially good." The next day he died from injuries received in the Iowa v. Minnesota football game.[18]

In November, George Shannon and attorney O.J. Smith organized a non-partisan St. Paul Colored Voters League which met at 1021 Colne Street. The League helped to increase colored voter turn-out and helped to pass laws to protect their rights. Shannon was also helping Frank Boyd organize Local #3 of the Brotherhood of Sleeping Car Porters (BSCP) and was subsequently elected its first president.

In December, an editorial in the *Appeal* noted that the reasons that Dr. Turner and Dr. Ossian Sweet of Detroit and our own W.T. Francis had wanted to move into better residential neighborhoods was not to obtain freer association with whites, but better housing, lighting and general living conditions which are all too often denied in African-American districts. Francis received the help of both Judge J.W. Willis and Dr. Valdo D. Turner in his fight to keep the property he had purchased at 2092 Sargent Street. They also helped Ernest Starks buy property at 2029 St. Clair Street.[19]

CHAPTER FIVE 1920 – 1929

In February 1924, W. T. Francis announced that a defense fund was being started for Max Mason, the unfortunate victim of Duluth mob justice, for his coming appearance before the state pardon board. Editor Howell, of the Northwestern Bulletin, said all names of contributors would be published on its front page.

Also that May, the St. Paul Equal Rights League petitioned President Coolidge to release the 54 soldiers of the 24th Infantry Division who had been accused of participating in the Houston Riots and were being held at Fort Levenworth.

Before the month was over the local NAACP reported that the prison sentences of all members of the regiment who had sought a reduction had been reduced. Eighteen were to be given their immediate release, sixteen would be eligible for release with the year, sixteen would be eligible for release in 1927 and the remaining four would be released in 1928.[20]

That fall, the Urban League proudly announced that in their first year of operation, it had succeeded in placing 240 of the 500 job applicants who had sought its assistance. Tom Arnold announced that he had been given the assignment of helping to organize a Mill City branch.

In October, National NAACP Director James Weldon Johnson made his first and only endorsement of a candidate when he gave his support to Robert M. LaFollette in the hope that African-American people would exploit the split in Republican ranks.[21]

The most significant boost to the Protest Tradition in St. Paul in the mid-twenties came when Earl Wilkins took over as full-time editor of the St. Paul Echo and soon became the dominant militant voice for the city's African-American community until he joined his brother Roy at the Kansas City Call in 1927.

Earl Wilkins never failed to rally his African-American subscribers when their rights were being threatened or failed to denounce the hypocrisy of local whites. He was a ubiquitous agitator who helped to revive the soul and spirit that J.Q. Adams had personified during his early years on the *Appeal*. Esther Bradley, who was a fledgling reporter at the time, stated that Wilkins was, "a real fighter who was as bright as a new silver dollar." Though he was plagued with recurring bouts of tuberculosis throughout his life, he always managed to make his mark as an uncompromising activist. He had been born in Holly Springs, Mississippi, in 1905, the son of the Reverend William DeWitt Wilkins and his wife, Mayfield. He was the third of three children and had an older brother, Roy, and an older sister, Armeda. Soon after his birth, their mother died and her sister, Elizabeth, with the approval of their father, took the three children back to St. Paul to be raised by her and her husband, Sam Williams. Earl Wilkins attended Whittier Elementary School, where he was a good student and won the Ramsey County Spelling Test for Seventh graders. In 1919, he entered Mechanic Arts High School and after graduation entered the University of Minnesota in 1921. As an upperclassman, he was hired part-time by Owen Howell, the editor of the St. Paul Echo, and in an early piece denounced President Coolidge for segregating the beaches in the nation's capitol.[22] He also declared the fact, to his readers, that the American Judicial system had managed to eliminate Marcus Garvey, their most effective leader, by sentencing him to five years of imprisonment on a trumped-up charge of mail fraud.

Wilkins bragged to his African-American readership about their Dr. J. W. Crump becoming the first local African-American physician to be admitted to the Ramsey County Medical Society, but also reminded them that African-American firefighter Nathaniel Evans, who had been next on the civil service list for fire captain, had been denied his promotion with the excuse that, "it would not be in the best interest of the department to promote a black man to command a white fire station."[23]

Wilkins, in an editorial that fall, praised the actions of the Twin City Urban League in their 18 months of continuous negotiations to secure job openings at the St. Paul Ford Plant and the success Elmer Carter had in finally getting Morris Goins, James Lee and William Shackleford hired.

In March 1926, Wilkins noted, on his pages, that there were still hostelries and eating places in St. Paul that would not serve "colored" patrons. He told his readers, "Let us resolve to stand firm and clear-eyes in our demands for our rights … Let us be men fighting and standing among men and be done with pretense and shameful acceptance."[24]

He went on to chastise African-American people for using the term, "nigger," among themselves and said no odium should be attached to it until we wipe the word out of our own vocabularies. He also went on to suggest that African-Americans have much to be proud of in their diversity and noted in an anonymous poem that:

Some of us are whiter than the average white person,
While others are a full yellow,
Still, other of us are light-brown,
And others are a golden brown,
Then others are a rich chocolate.
You can find still others of us who are fairly red,
And many who are black, blue-black, purple-black and even a silent dry black.
But, all of us are beautiful and there is no good reason
for us to practice color prejudice within our own group.
The sooner we develop a greater unity, the sooner we
will find both greater understanding and success.

He informed his readers that Manufacturer's Record had declared that 10.5 million African-Americans in America had accumulated over 1.5 billion dollars in wealth and that they were producing 1,000 college graduates annually, that they made up 14 percent of all iron and steel workers, 10 percent of all railroad workers and that they operated 1 million farms of which 250,000 were owner-occupied.[25]

In November, Wilkins alerted his readers that the St. Paul Hotel had refused proper accommodations for black America's "Prince of Preachers," the Reverend Charles A. Tindley of Philadelphia. His temple was the largest African Methodist Episcopal Church in America, with seven assistant pastors and almost ten thousand members. Tindley composed such famous hymns as "The Storm is Passing Over," "We'll Understand it Better By and By" and the ever popular, "Stand By Me." He became known as the "Father of American Hymnody" and three decades after his death, was the subject of a doctoral Dissertation by the Rev. Amos Brown, who had at one time served as pastor of St. Paul's Pilgrim Baptist Church. Wilkins raged at the humiliation the 76-year-old Tindley must have felt for having to use the freight elevator to get to his rooms during his winter visit.[26]

In January 1927, a more serious and potentially fatal form of discrimination took place when Mrs. Herman Lewis called Ancker Hospital for an ambulance at one o'clock in the morning for her husband who had been stricken with acute abdominal pains shortly after midnight. The hospital refused to send an ambulance, as did the city police department, and she was unable to get a cab to take him until 3 o'clock that morning.[27]

In February 1927, Wilkins reminded his readers that the Wilder Baths were still segregated despite the wishes of the man who had bequeathed them to the city and also complained about the continuing segregation of the YMCA pool and noted that, "no other group in the city, of similar economic circumstances, contribute as much to the Community Chest as do the colored community". He also noted that both the Wilder Baths and the YMCA had been exempted from a normal tax burden of $300,000 while the African-American community's tax burden had increased and their exemption was, "greater than the value of all the Negro-owned houses on St. Anthony, from Western Avenue to Grotto Street."[28]

CHAPTER FIVE 1920 – 1929

In March, Wilkins suggested that if the African-American community wanted economic security they could achieve it through cooperation. He suggested that if all members of the 1,200 African-American families who lived in the area bounded by Rice and Oxford Streets and Thomas and Iglehart Avenues would spend just two dollars a week at the two African-American grocery stores in the area it would increase their incomes by $2,400.[29]

The following summer, the Echo proudly announced that it was offering for sale parcels of land for summer occupancy at Minesure, a 280-acre resort area located about five miles from Hastings and two miles north of Point Douglas. It also stated that payments for lots could be made at their office at 614 Court Block and could extend over a five-year period. Attorney James A. Harris and Business Manager Cyrus Lewis handled legal matters.

The following November, Republican Oscar DePriest also became the first African-American elected to the Congress since 1901 as well as the first to be elected from a Northern state. He had been selected by Mayor William Hale Thompson from Chicago's Second Ward to represent the First Congressional District, which had an 80 percent African-American vote. He had previously served as a County Commissioner from 1904–08 and Alderman from 1915-17. He was elected by a 3,000 vote majority. One of his first civil rights achievements was to make the Washington, D.C. Auditorium available for African-American organizations.

In January 1929, Urban League Executive Director Robert Smalls demanded that radio station KSTP discontinue its use of the words, "pickaninny and nigger" while introducing African-American melodies, and received an apology and a promise from its assistant manager that their use would be discontinued.

The following month, Smalls recommended to his board that they formally protest to the Salvation Army Men's Shelter at 53 W. Third

Street, their refusal to house an African-American man on the 21st of the month.

In March, in his inaugural address, President Herbert Hoover stated that he would be President of all the people and though he did not appoint any Southerners to his Cabinet, he also failed to appoint any African-Americans to his fact-finding committee on law enforcement. His predecessor Calvin Coolidge had made a truly significant appointment when he replaced Solomon Hood with W.T. Francis as Minister to Liberia. It was a well-deserved honor that unfortunately, he and Nellie were unable to enjoy as the following summer he was stricken with Yellow Fever and died at the age of 60 on June 15th. He left a rich civil rights legacy to the 4,000 plus African-American citizens of St. Paul as well as honor to the entire state.[30]

That spring, the St. Paul Urban League had not only opened the doors to the St. Paul Ford Plant for African-American workers, but had also secured jobs at the American Radiator Plant and the Lowry Hotel as part of its placement of over 400 applicants in a variety of jobs, throughout the city since the previous year.[31]

On May 30th, Smalls became the first African-American veteran to participate in the American Legion's School Program and the following month he was able to send the first African-American female to the YWCA's Lake Geneva Summer Camp.

That fall, Urban League board member, Dr. W.F. Ryder offered a course in "Negro History" at Macalester College, which used Carter Woodson's "The Negro in America" as its text.

The decade left the state with the dreadful legacy of a triple lynching in Duluth, but also the successful passage of a state anti-lynching law. It was also a period which finally embraced the right of women to vote as well as the state's first African-American woman to pass the state bar examination. The decade brought the Twin Cities their first Urban League, which was to champion the cause of widening employment opportunities and social progress for both cities. The city profited from the efforts of the Wilkins brothers who made an impact locally as well as nationally on the cause of civil rights. One of the most significant civil rights gains of the 1920s was the U.S. Supreme Court's decision, in 1927, in Nixon v. Herndon, which made the barring of African-Americans from Texas Primaries illegal, but the slight gains it made paled in the light of the Court's decision that year to uphold the Eugenic laws of 30 states which eventually permitted the sterilization of over 60,000 African-Americans for mental illness, retardation, epilepsy, alcoholism or immorality. It was 1974 before Virginia, the last state with such laws, finally repealed them.[32]

CHAPTER FIVE BIBLIOGRAPHY

1. *Appeal,* 10 January 1920.

2. Fedo, Michael W., *They was Just Niggers; An Account of One of the Nation's Least Known Tragedies,* Brasch and Brasch Publishers, Inc., Ontario, California, 1979, p. 114.

3. *St. Paul Pioneer Press,* 22 February 1998.

4. Spangler, Earl, *The Negro in Minnesota* p. 102

5. Fedo, Michael W., *They was Just Niggers,* p. 35.

6. ibid.. p. 168

7. *Appeal,* 11 December 1920.

8. *Appeal,* 30 April 1921.

9. *Appeal,* 2 July 1921.

10. *Minneapolis Tribune,* 29 February 2000.

11. *Appeal,* 22 October 1921.

    Madigan, Tim, *The Burning; Massacre, Destruction, and the Tulsa Riot of 1921,* Thomas Dunne Books, St. Martin Press, New York, 2001, pp. 221-222, 230.

12. *Appeal,* 3 December 1921.

13. *Appeal,* 10 December 1922.

14. *Appeal,* 7 July 1923.

15. *Appeal,* 23 September 1923.

16. *Appeal,* 11 August 1923.

17. *Appeal,* 13 October 1923.

18. *Appeal,* 20 October 1923.

19. *Appeal,* 6 December 1923.

20. *Appeal*, 31 May 1924.

21. Johnson, James Weldon, "The Gentlemen's Agreement and the Negro Vote," *Crisis Magazine*, October 1924.

22. *St. Paul Echo*, 5 March 1925.

23. Griffin, James, *Blacks in the St. Paul Fire Department: 1885–1976*, E and J Publishing, St. Paul, Minnesota, 1976, p. 36.

24. *St. Paul Echo*, 27 March 1926.

25. *St. Paul Echo*, 12 July 1926.

26. *St. Paul Echo*, 28 November 1926.

27. *St. Paul Echo*, 8 January 1927.

28. *St. Paul Echo*, 12 February 1927.

29. *St. Paul Echo*, 12 March 1927.

30. *St. Paul Recorder*, 5 June 1980.

31. *St. Paul Echo*, 16 April 1929.

32. *Minneapolis Star-Tribune*, 15 February 2001.

Chapter Six
1930 – 1939

CECIL NEWMAN: HEIR TO THE PROTEST TRADITION

"I shall be an advocate for these human and civil rights on behalf of those to whom they are denied and I shall turn the pitiless light of publicity upon all those who would deny those rights to others..."

Editor P. Bernard Young, Norfolk Journal and Guide, 1944.

The man who was destined to become the Twin Cities leading civil rights agitator, advocate and activist of the Protest Tradition for the next half century was born in Kansas City, Missouri, in July, 1903. Being the only boy in a family of three girls, Cecil Newman soon became their favorite and his early family recollections were pleasant ones. His father, Horatio, prided himself for never having been on relief even during the worst days of the Depression. He had begun work as an attendant at a private club, but after Cecil was born, he had worked his way up to being a chef at one of Kansas City's finest hotels.

However, Cecil became aware of the evils of prejudice at the age of seven when his playmate's mother told him that, "The reason you can't attend Mary's school is because you're a nigger."

As a young boy, Cecil had a great interest in reading, and was fortunate in inheriting the rather extensive library of a deceased family head for whom his mother had worked. The widow had given Cecil's mother over four hundred books to help nurture his love of learning. When he was twelve, Cecil decided one day to put on a circus and recruited his young friend, Langston Hughes, to do his magic act. The circus was a huge success and when Cecil and Langston headed for the local amusement park to celebrate, they were told "Negroes" were not allowed.

Cecil Newman

Cecil's curiosity caused him to investigate the history of Swope Park and he found that the tract of land had been bequeathed to the city with the stipulation that it was to remain unsegregated. Cecil brought it to the attention of the editor of the local African-American newspaper who aroused the wrath of the African-American community and the park was desegregated.

One of Cecil's first jobs was as an office boy with the Kansas City Call, an African-American weekly. During his senior year, Cecil was able to get a complaint printed in the Call that though the city had a few African-American principals in their schools there was no African-American administrator at the central office. Cecil was called to his principal's office the next Monday and was reprimanded for "stirring things up." A fellow student encouraged him to be a journalist, and later when he read the life of Elijah Lovejoy, a journalist who had given his life for the right to speak out against racial injustice and intolerance, he decided this was to be his future vocation.

After a variety of jobs and an early marriage to Willa Colman in his junior year, Cecil Newman graduated, and arrived in Kansas City in 1922 with $1.27 in his pockets. Newman's first job was that of a waiter at the African-American Elks Club.

In 1924, he began work selling subscriptions for the Northwestern Bulletin. Before long he began working as a "stringer" or freelance writer for the Pittsburgh Courier and the Chicago Defender and occasionally had an article printed.

Before long, he met Joshua Perry, a freelance printer, who was to help further his ambitions. Newman then decided to form a corporation with Joseph Levy, a railroader, Dutch Thomason, a bar owner, J. Edward

Stewart, a night club owner, and businessmen Robert Moulden and Marvin Shivers. All six had a combined capital of $2,000. By April, Newman had relocated to the Twin Cities and the *Twin City Herald* had published its first edition and the 24 year-old's first editorial was written on the efforts to reduce crime in the African-American community and the need to combat police brutality. In a later editorial in the *Twin City Herald*, in 1930, Editor Newman noted that African-Americans scored perhaps their first truly significant national political victory when their opposition to the confirmation of Judge John H. Parker to the U.S. Supreme Court was strong enough for President Hoover to withdraw his name. Parker's long suspected strong "anti-Negro" attitudes had become the subject of repeated protests by many African-American groups including both national and local NAACP chapters who had continually lobbied against his confirmation in the U.S. Senate. Their efforts helped to defeat over 11 U.S. senators who had supported Parker.

During the early 1930's, Cecil continued his struggle to put out a newspaper while working as a Pullman porter. The owners of the *Twin City Herald* now owed him over five thousand dollars in wages. Joshua Perry agreed to let Cecil publish a Time and Literary Digest magazine in lieu of some of his past wages. The first edition of his Time and Literary Digest was only 8 1/2" x 11" and sold for 15 cents and he dedicated it to, "Covering the worth-while activities of Afro-Americans rather than just the sensational crimes as did white magazines."[1]

In June, Robert Smalls, the Executive Secretary of the St. Paul Urban League, reported to his membership the results of a survey taken the previous year by Dr. Walter S. Ryder, of Macalester College. He found that the African-American population of the city was approximately 4,000 or 1.8 percent of the city's total population and were predominately located in Wards 7, 8, 9 and 12. They had an average of 3.4 members per household. He also found that 20 percent of the African-American population were southern migrants and was surprised to find that 48 percent owned their own homes and 25 percent of the mothers worked outside of their homes. His survey also pointed out the pervasive job discrimination within the city. Of the 90 firms visited only 1 laundry out of 34 employed African-Americans and 72 said they would not even consider employing them. Only two firms had African-American employees who were union members, and of the 870 African-American employees surveyed, almost half, or 420, were employed by the railroads and an additional 20 percent by two packing plants. 90 were self-employed while 60 were employed in city and county jobs and 30 worked in hotels and mens' clubs.[2] Dr. Ryder concluded his survey by commending the League for successfully placing 50 workers during the preceding year and with the observation that the African-American community in St. Paul was beginning to resemble one which Alain Locke described in his New Negro, "as a community which had become a conscious contributor rather than merely a beneficiary and was assuming that of a collaborator and participant in our American civilization."[3]

About this time, Mrs. Nellie Griswold Francis, the widow of the late Minister to Liberia, told the NAACP that she had been denied her husband's yearly salary, which had previously been granted to the widows of the U.S. Foreign Service. The payment was to have been $5,000, but it had been objected to by U.S. Representative William H. Stafford of Milwaukee on the grounds that the claim had failed to list Mrs. Francis as a dependent and because the measure had not been specifically included in the recently re-negotiated salary agreements, which had been reached after his death. In the agreement, Stafford argued, it had specifically stated that payment should not be given retroactively. Mrs. Francis concluded that the congressional nit-picking had been racially motivated and requested that her legal counsel continue to pursue the matter.[4]

That winter, Owen Howell, the president of the St. Paul Negro Civic League, and Louis Ervin, who had been assigned to the case by the St. Paul Urban League, met with Clyde L. May, the city's Commissioner of Parks and Playgrounds on behalf of Thomas Lewis who had been dismissed from his job. After a number of negotiation sessions, which took place between September and Christmas, Ervin was able to prove that Lewis had been unfairly dismissed and had had an excellent job rating over the preceding 16 years.[5]

Monitor Editor William Helm, also noted that 20 African-Americans had been lynched the previous year but told his readers he had been encouraged by the fact that 17 whites had been indicted, last November, for the lynching of Allen Green, an African-American from Oconee County, South Carolina. The Monitor's poll of St. Paul railroad wives found that the tips of Pullman porters and waiters in 1930 were only half what they had been in 1929 and had taken their biggest drop since Prohibition had gone into effect in 1918. Pullman porter's wages were still $25 per month.[6]

The following year, St. Paulites won a mild legal victory with the appointment of Mrs. Doris Roper of 982 Fuller Ave. as the city's first African-American woman to serve on a Ramsey County Grand Jury.[7]

St. Paul lost one of its most talented professionals in 1931, when Grace Lealtad left her teaching post at Jackson Elementary School to take a better paying teaching position in Gary, Indiana. The St. Paul NAACP, disheartened by her resignation, held a mass meeting of parents of both Maxfield and McKinley Schools to protest the conditions which brought about her resignation and also the continuing absence of Parent-Teacher Associations at either of the city's predominantly black elementary schools. Clarence Darrow was their guest speaker. Their president, Dr. Valdo Turner, appointed Mary Coombs, Marie Hyde, Eva Neal and Myrtle Carden, Hallie Q. Brown Community House Director, to investigate the matter and report back.

Cecil Newman's May issue of his Timely Digest had a feature story on one of the most celebrated miscarriages of justice in the nation's history. It was an article he wrote condemning the indictment of the nine Scottsboro Boys. The most significant result of the subsequent trial and conviction of the boys came about when the United States Supreme Court reversed their convictions in a precedent-setting ruling. It was based on the fact that African-Americans had been systematically denied the right to serve on juries throughout the entire history of the state of Alabama and that the boys had thus been denied "due process" under the Fifth Amendment.

In June, Cecil Newman was asked by President J.W. Baldwin of the Brotherhood of Sleeping Car Porters (BSCP) to serve as chairman of the negotiations between the Brotherhood and the Soo Line Railroad. The Brotherhood was attempting to organize the porters and their request showed the deep respect they had for Newman's negotiating abilities.

Roy Wilkins, after leaving St. Paul, worked eight years on the Kansas City Call, five of them with his brother, Earl. During the fall of 1931, Walter White appointed Wilkins Assistant Secretary of the National NAACP. He soon discovered that African-Americans were facing overwhelming odds that year in the area of employment.

In the spring of 1932, Wilkins had 10,000 copies of a leaflet called Mississippi River Slavery published by the NAACP. It gave the results of a study he and George Schuyler had made on the conditions which existed on the federal flood-control work projects in that state. The working conditions were so bad that a Senate investigations committee decided after its hearings that they would recommend setting up minimum wage standards for all workers in America.

In June, attorney Lena O. Smith was successful in winning a civil suit for $1,000 for African-American worker, Tom Cash, of St. Paul, who had been brutally beaten by a Great Northern special policeman. She later won an additional $2,000 for her client.[8]

Also in July of that year, the beloved Father Stephen Theobald died at the age of 58. He had been one of only four ordained black Catholic priests in the United States. After his assignment to the St. Peter Claver Parish, he had set about raising money to equip its sanctuary with three white marble alters as well as a large mural which depicted Saint Peter Claver administering to his followers. Father Theobald contributed $1,000 to the purchase of the first pipe organ for the church. The church served as the official Shrine of St. Theresa de Liseux, which became known as "The Little Flower."

Theobald worked hard in the field of civil rights and was active in the St. Paul NAACP for two decades and also served as the spiritual advisor for The Committee Against the Extension of Race Prejudice.

This group made use of the Catholic press to support its efforts to combat racial prejudice at both the St. Paul Seminary and local parishes throughout the archdiocese. Later the committee became a branch of the Federated Colored Catholics of America. Theobald was uncompromising in his condemnation of Catholic apologists and fence-straddlers who took ambiguous positions on African-American rights and was even more strongly critical of some politically-minded bishops who waffled on the subject of racial justice. His courageous approach gained him considerable stature among many African-American Catholics. In 1931, at the Annual Convention of the Federated Colored Catholics, in St. Louis, Missouri, he gave a keynote address entitled, "Our Hopes and Aspirations." In his speech, he insisted that the Catholic Church should combat all forms of discrimination and should insist that all Catholics receive the "essentials of life and respect for the Immortality of all human souls." He not only attacked the color line at St. Louis University, but deplored all segregated Catholic institutions which he denounced as being un-Christian. He particularly pointed out the practices of Catholic hospitals that received non-Catholic white patients, but refused to admit African-American Catholic patients. The speech further endeared him to African-American Catholics throughout the nation and thereafter his parish in St. Paul became a Mecca for special Catholic services on racial matters. This diminutive but courageous priest was accepted by both Protestant and Catholic groups in the Twin Cities and he continued to be a confessor for both Catholic clergy and the sisters of the diocese.

That summer after celebrating his 22nd anniversary at St. Peter Claver, he was suddenly stricken with a ruptured appendix. By the time the appendectomy was performed, peritonitis had set in and he lingered for only four days. During that time, Archbishop Murray was constantly at his bedside and on July 12 Theobald slipped into a coma. The national Catholic weekly, America, eulogized him by saying, "his life and character were a refutation to those who would deny the honors of the church to members of the Negro race." He was buried in Calvary Cemetery on July 18, 1932.

Near the end of the year, St. Paul's congressman, Melvin Mass became somewhat of a hero to the African-American community by introducing a bill in the U.S. House of Representatives which compensated Mrs. W.T. Francis for the pension the U.S. State Department had so long denied her.[9]

On January 14, 1933, a memorial service was held to honor Thomas H. Lyles, the business leader who had been instrumental in not only helping to found the African-American community's fourth estate, but also Engine Company #9 in 1885. He had also been instrumental in bringing about the appointment of St. Paul's first African-American policemen, James Burrel, in 1892. Jose Sherwood delivered the main eulogy on the 13th anniversary of his passing.

That summer, the *Twin City Herald* berated the African-American community for allowing Ernie Fowler's death at the county workhouse to go unchallenged. Fowler, had been arrested and charged with disorderly conduct, but had died at Ancker Hospital from the treatment he had received after his incarceration.[10]

In August, Newman continued his campaign against employment discrimination and it resulted in the employment of Rudy Martin as a clerk at McGowan's Drugstore on Grotto and Rondo Streets. Soon after that the St. Paul Urban League set up an employment office at 419 Wabasha Street and continued to support the *Herald*'s campaign to collect letters of protest from those African-Americans in St. Paul who had been laid-off because their employers refused to meet the National Recovery Act pay guidelines.[11]

By the end of the year, Newman severed his connections with the *Herald*, and struck out on his own to found a newspaper.

In January 1934, Roy Wilkins, for the second time in just over a decade, publicly denounced prejudice in Big Ten athletics. This time it was against the actions of University of Michigan's basketball coach, Frank Cappon, for refusing to play All-American center Franklin Lett because of an "unwritten agreement" between Big Ten coaches not to play African-American members of their teams when they played southern colleges. Wilkins in his capacity as the Assistant Secretary of the National NAACP remembered his days as editor of the University of Minnesota's Minnesota Daily when he had protested the same type of actions and had reminded Cappon then, that the University of Michigan was a state-supported institution. He had also written in his editorial of Cappon's, "gross ingratitude to the black tax-payers of his state of Michigan who helped buy his salary."[12]

Two months later, African-American St. Paulites were pleased to hear that their state's House delegation had supported Representative Oscar DePriest's petition to allow African-Americans to use the House Dining Room. The matter later passed the full House by a vote of 237–113 with 79 abstentions.[13]

In April, both St. Paulites as well as the nation, were shocked to learn that William Monroe Trotter had fallen or had leaped to his death from his apartment in his three-story home in Boston. During the first two decades of the twentieth century, Trotter had been a bold and brilliant activist, who had given his unstinting support to the Protest movement. He has been born on April 7, 1872, in Chillicothe, Ohio, where he received his early education and had been elected president of his senior high-school class. He went on to earn a B.A. degree, Magna Cum Laude, from Harvard, in 1895, and the following year an M.A., which resulted in his becoming the nation's first African-American member of the Phi Beta Kappa Society. In 1901, he began publishing the Boston Guardian and soon became a crusading editor who founded The National Equal Right League. He had also had been one of the first to challenge the racist policies of both Presidents Theodore Roosevelt and Taft and had personally confronted President Wilson at a White House Conference and verbally castigated him for his segregationist policies before Wilson abruptly adjourned the conference and had Trotter ejected from the White House and banned forever from the premises. This did not stop Trotter from chastising President Coolidge in 1926 over his segregation policies nor diminish his unswerving commitment to the causes of equal justice, despite great personal sacrifice.

After the city general election that spring, the *Herald* pointed out to Mayor William Mahoney that if he had been a little more sensitive to the needs of African-Americans in the community and if he had given a qualified African-American a position of importance in his administration he might still be mayor.[14]

In November, Democrat Arthur Mitchell defeated Oscar De Priest by 3,130 votes. He became the first African-American Democrat elected in the history of the House of Representatives.

About this time, Roy Wilkins was asked to take over as editor of the Crisis Magazine from W.E.B. DuBois, who resigned because of differences in policies and racial strategies with those of the NAACP's Board of Directors. While they were advocating desegregation, DuBois was proposing the establishment of cooperative commonwealths within the nation's African-American communities along with the socialization of African-American professional services, which frightened many of the African-American bourgeoisie. DuBois felt that if the purchasing power of 13 million African-Americans could be concentrated in consumer cooperatives they could raise the economic status of all African-Americans as well as their self-esteem.

An event occurred near the end of the year, which probably created a greater impetus to the cause of civil rights in the Twin Cities than any other event during the next four decades. It was the decision by Cecil Newman to publish his own weekly newspaper. He was assisted in the endeavor by William Smith, his associate editor, Arthur Allen, his advertising manager, Nell Dodson, his sole columnist, and Robert Jones, a sales representative in St. Paul.

Certainly one of the major events of the year was the publishing of Newman's weekly newspaper whose first edition had the paper's credo, which read, "THE MINNESOTA SPOKESMAN and the ST. PAUL RECORDER believe that no man should be denied the right to contribute his best to humanity. As long as that right is denied any man, no man's rights are inviolate." Newman was able to get his paper started by raising his initial funds from a job he had been offered as advertising manager for the Kansas City Call in St. Louis, Missouri. He was paid a salary of $100 a week and managed to live on $25 dollars a week. He sent $25 to his wife and the remainder to William Smith to pay the cost for producing the paper. During his five-month absence, the *Recorder* continued to be published, but upon his return he found that he owed Andersen and Foss Typesetting Company $5,200.[15]

One of the ways he decided he could help pay his debts was to expand his advertising to those white businesses, which had a vested interest in the African-American community. This feat thrust Newman into the role of a civic leader as well as a new voice to carry on the Protest Tradition begun a half century ago.

In November, the Brotherhood of Sleeping Car Porters appealed to B'nai Bri'th to help them have a sign removed from Carol Gorkin's saloon, on Seventh and Jackson Streets, near the Union Depot, which said, "No colored trade solicited." Newman convinced Mr. Gorkin to change his attitude and the sign was removed and a letter of apology was sent to the Brotherhood of Sleeping Car Porters's Secretary-Treasurer, Frank Boyd.

Beginning in January 1935, the *Spokesman-Recorder* started a policy of listing business firms who hired blacks while urging its readers to boycott those who did not. It resulted in St. Phillips Episcopal Church and the Reverend Victor Holly to cancel his church picnic order from Hamm's Brewery and giving it instead to Yankee Brewery, because they employed African-American drivers. When Newman received reports that the Pilot of Freeman Airways, Nels Swanson, was refusing to take African-American people up on sight-seeing trips from Holman Field. He called a department store owner, who held considerable stock in the company. He ordered the pilot to show the same courtesies to African-American passengers as he showed whites.

In February, Newman editorialized that the *St. Paul Dispatch* and *Pioneer Press* and the *St. Paul Daily News* were still refusing to capitalize the word Negro and suggested that Woodson's Negro History Week would be a good time for them to change their policies.

That fall, Dwight Reed, who wore the Gopher's number twenty six and was an All-American End candidate on the University of Minnesota's football team, was ordered by Coach Bierman to sit-out the Tulane game and act as a spotter in a radio booth, above Memorial Stadium. Bierman claimed he was simply complying with the unwritten agreement among Big Ten and southern coaches to bench their colored players when playing southern teams. It was a policy, which Roy Wilkins had vehemently protested as editor of the Minnesota Daily.[16]

In the spring of 1936, Miss Margaret Benjamin, a music education major at the University of Minnesota, was told by her instructor that he would not be able to place her as a practice-teacher. She contacted Mr. C.W. Washington, of the St. Paul Urban League, who took her to see Education Commissioner Pearce, who secured her an assignment.[17]

That June, General Mills, whose major product was the cereal "Wheaties" brought their favorite sports announcer, Byrum Saam to broadcast the Olympic try-outs at the University's Memorial Stadium. During his broadcast, Saam repeatedly referred to Frederick "Fritz" Pollard, an African-American player on Walter Camp's All-American Football Team, as a "nigger" during his broadcasts. Editor Newman took both Saam and General Mills to task and demanded an apology, and the following week received one from both the University and the Big Ten Officials.[18]

In July, Newman berated Salvation Army Commander Colonel Pensold for declaring publicly that there would be separate summer camps for white and African-American children, after years of integration. However, after meeting with Newman, he changed his mind and said he now favored an integrated encampment.[19]

In August, Newman printed a poem:

FUNNY WHITE FOLKS

They began by stealing us from Africa and ended up by condemning us for stealing.

They began by forcing us to go to work and ended up not allowing us to work.

They began by taking our females and ended up by lynching us for looking at theirs.

They began by ridiculing our songs and dances and ended up imitating them.

They began by cursing our gambling and ended up by adopting it.

They began by laughing at our brown skins and ended up by using the sun to give themselves the same kind.

They began by promising us heaven and ended up by giving us hell.

November was marked by the formation of a St. Paul Interracial Committee which sponsored a conference at St. Catherine's College, in St. Paul. The main speaker was the Reverend John LaFarge, who earlier that year had formed the nation's first Catholic Interracial Council, which helped bring Catholics into the field of better interracial and multicultural understanding. In his address, LaFarge stressed that prejudice could best be overcome by personal contact and the joint discussion of common problems.

A positive gain, which had been made that year for African-Americans, was the appointment of Mary McLeod Bethune by President Roosevelt, which made her the national director of the Negro Division of the National Youth Administration and the first African-American woman to head a federal office. Later, she was instrumental in creating an informal "Black Cabinet" of distinguished African-American leaders with whom the President Roosevelt sometimes conferred.

Cecil Newman was pleased to discover that subscription to both his papers had increased and concluded it was because they were serving a dual public. On the one hand, he was publishing the news of the African-American communities and including their social affairs in his pages as well as their vital statistics. He felt that a second purpose he was performing was in keeping members of the white communities apprised of African-American achievement taking place in their businesses, their educational facilities and in sports. He also made it a practice to re-print articles from other African-American weeklies such as the Chicago Defender, the Pittsburgh Courier, and the Baltimore Afro-American as well as other white and minority owned dailies. He felt that too often African-American news that found its way into white dailies was of a sensational nature and he felt that more positive news would not only raise the morale of his African-American readers, but also make his white readers better informed as to what was really taking place in the whole African-American community.

That summer, at the Republican Party Convention their platform vowed, "We pledge our protection of the Negro's economic status and personal safety…" The Crisis magazine, however, condemned the pledge as being, "precisely what the Negroes do not want, DuBois contended that the Negro's present economic status was the chief cause of his discontent." The NAACP endorsed Roosevelt because, "he has done more for the Negro economically, than any Republican President since Lincoln…"

Early in 1937, William Henry Hastie was nominated by President Roosevelt to become America's first African-American Federal District Court Judge. Unfortunately, he was assigned to serve in the Virgin Islands, which attests to the cautious liberalism of F.D.R. Hastie was 32-years-old and had been born in Knoxville, Tennessee, where he received his early education. He later attended Amherst College where he earned a B.A. degree. When he was 22-years-old, he entered Harvard Law School where he earned both L.L.B. and S.J.D. degrees. After leaving Harvard, in 1930, he joined the faculty of Howard University where he taught until his appointment.

That February, Editor Newman suggested to 25 Twin City ministers that they pledge 50 cents a week to advertise in his *Spokesman-Recorder*. He was disappointed to find that only eight responded to his request and only seven took out an ad though eight offered him spiritual support. The other seventeen asked him for additional time to study his request.[20]

That spring, one of St. Paul's earliest Catholic civil rights activists addressed the American Inter-Professional Institute. Father Francis J. Gilligan was instructor of sociology and moral theology at St. Paul's Catholic Seminary. After recounting many examples of racial discrimination faced by St. Paul's African-American population, he startled his audience by declaring, "If I were a colored man and not a Christian, I imagine I would be very receptive towards the attitudes of the Soviet government toward race." For the remainder of the decade, Gilligan continued to be outspoken and contentious.[21]

Later that spring another man of the cloth, the Reverend Lee W. Harris, led over 300 members of the Twin City Ministerial Alliance to the state capitol where he addressed the Senate. He spoke of many concerns of the state's African-American citizens and concluded by admonishing the Senate and the House for employing only 232 African-American citizens throughout the entire state government work force out of a total of 1,600.[22]

In June, Frank Boyd, the local organizer of the Brotherhood of Sleeping Car Porters (BSCP) was gratified to hear that their national

Frank Boyd

headquarters had been offered International Charter #18078 by the American Federation of Labor. It inspired Boyd to work even harder to add to Local #3's 240 members. Boyd joined with Frank Alsop of the Packing House Workers to organize the Minnesota Negro Labor Council, which they formed to combat employment discrimination and to promote the employment interests of African-Americans. Clifford E. Rucker was their first chairman and his major political objective was to organize a lobbying effort for the passage of the Wagner-Van Mayo Anti-Lynching Bill. Boyd was pleased when the Pullman Company finally agreed to formally recognize the BSCP on the first of October and to provide porters with two million dollars in long overdue pay raises. It served as a catalyst for Boyd's organizing efforts and also helped him to build his division into one of the strongest in the nation.

Editor Newman asked his readers to join his Friendly Merchant Consumer Club to work against employment discrimination that was being practiced by white proprietors and lending institutions. He noted that the two African-American communities had spent almost $3.5 million with area merchants who had few or no African-American employ-ees.[23]

Newman also urged the newly independent St. Paul Urban League to be careful to employ a staff, "who will act as servants of the public rather than as public supervisors and to choose their executive boards from all classes of people and not just the middle-class." He said, "They should reflect all shades of opinion and to be sure to eliminate any white board members who give only lip-service to opportunities for Negroes and fail to practice what they preach."[24]

On June 22, the nation's African-American community had celebrat-ed the victory of Joe Louis in his championship bout with James J. Braddock. Less than a week later, however, the community was sad-dened, by the passing of 80-year-old John Hickman, who had arrived in St. Paul in 1863 with his father, Robert. Hickman had been only six years old when his father had established Pilgrim Baptist Church on the corner of Wabasha and Third Streets, along with charter members Fielding Combs, Henry Moffit, John Trotter and Giles Crenshaw.

In July, the Urban League protested the policy of the Civilian Conservation Corps for refusing to register African-American men from the Twin Cities because of their policy of separate quotas for African-Americans and whites. The *Recorder* urged African-Americans to write their congressman to change the policy and the separate system was can-celed by the end of the month.[25]

The following summer, Lou Ervin was successful in getting Burnett Godman paroled from St. Cloud Reformatory. Godman's family had spent eleven years trying to find a lawyer they could afford. Two months later, Ervin was able to get Godman a job at the Grand Central Food Market.[26]

Editor Newman also reminded his readers that if they thought they were doing well politically, they should remember that only one African-American served on the state central committee of either major party.

He also noted that both Senators Lundeen and Shipstead had done an about-face on the Wagner-Van Nuys Anti-Lynching Bill with Lundeen voting against it on the first ballot and Shipstead voting against cloture when it was being filibustered.

During the summer session at the University of Minnesota, Newman began an aggressive campaign to desegregate the student dormitories. St. Paul student leaders Bea Schuck, Charlotte Crump, and Helen Hilyer assisted him in his efforts. Together, they got the matter before the University's Board of Regents and were able to convince Dean Guy Stanton Ford that a new non-discriminatory policy for student housing was badly needed.

Newman continued to castigate F.D.R. for having the audacity to offer the ten million citizens of Canada protection from foreign powers while he was unwilling to guarantee the same protection to ten million of his own African-American citizens from being lynched. He noted that, "If charity begins at home surely Negroes should share his magnanimity."[27]

During State Fair Week, activist Cliff Rucker brought charges of discrimination against the Lutheran Church booth and other eating concessions at the State Fair for posting signs saying, "Colored Trade, Not Solicited." Newman came to Rucker's aid, which prompted Fair Director, Raymond Lee, to finally order the signs removed. The incident prompted Newman to print Section 7321 of the Minnesota Civil Rights Law on the front page of the *Recorder* for the next several months with the admonition, "THE LAW IS VERY PLAIN USE IT!"[28]

That fall, Louis Ervin, who was president of the Minnesota Political League, exulted when the U.S. Supreme Court had declared in the New Negro Alliance v. Grocery Company decision that, "the picketing of firms, which refused to hire Negroes was a legal technique for securing redress." He also noted that the NAACP's challenge to include African-

American Scouts in the National Jamboree in Washington, D.C. had been successful.

In October, with the ending of a successful Saint's baseball season, Newman chided St. Paulites for not getting more upset with the exclusion of African-American players not only from AAA baseball, but also the major leagues. He noted in an editorial that in Chicago, African-American patrons spent over $20,000 a season at Wrigley Field, despite the fact that when Chicago sportscaster Bob Elson, asked the Sox star first baseman, Jake Powell, how he kept in shape during the off-season he had replied, "Oh, that's easy, I'm a policeman and I beat niggers over their heads with my blackjack!" As a result of his admission, African-American patrons decided to have milk-less Saturdays until the company who sponsored Elson employed African-American workers.[29]

In November, Clarence Mitchell was hired as Executive Secretary for the St. Paul Urban League. He was from Baltimore and had received a B.A. from the Lincoln University, had completed a fellowship from the Atlanta School for Social Work and a stint as a National Youth Administrator in Atlanta.

When the newly elected Governor, Harold Stassen, entered office on January 3, 1939, he immediately set about firing several African-Americans on the Capitol office staff, with the exception of Aides Billy Williams and George Hoage, who had served ten state governors before him and Andrew Owens, who was a clerk in the unemployment division. One of the first fired was Clifford Rucker, who headed the state's relief agency, which was perhaps the most responsible position then held by anyone of color in state government.[30]

Later that month, fireman Nathanial Evans filed a suit against Commissioner of Public Safety Gus Barfus for attempting to discharge him without a civil service hearing. Evans, who had been first appointed in 1918, had incurred the wrath of some public officials in 1925 when he complained for having been denied his promotion to captain because there was no opening at that time at an African-American station. He noted that now when a white fireman had topped the civil service list for captain and there had been no opening for him at a white station, he had been assigned to African-American Engine Company # 9. When this happened, Evans wrote, in a letter to the *Recorder*, "Some Negroes in St. Paul are celebrating the end of a segregated station. I would certainly like to differ with them, as I believe the appointment of white Captain, Harry Scott, to replace black Captain Davenport at Engine Company # 9 is not a victory but a defeat. Why is it when the cat comes to live at the home of the mice some mice shout and clap their hands with glee because they are so happy they have finally made a friend of the cat? They forget that a cat is always a cat and cats eat mice! To say that Scott helped to end segregation is simply to forget the fact that a white man got a black man's job."[31]

The following month, the St. Paul Urban League sponsored a Waiters Clinic at the YMCA with 40 men in attendance. By the end of the month the St. Paul and the Lowry Hotels had hired most of the clinic's graduates. The League's Executive Secretary, Clarence Mitchell, was also able to convince State Senator B.G. Novak to introduce a bill in the Minnesota Legislature, which provided that, "No insurance company or its agents shall refuse to issue policies of insurance or practice discrimination in the acceptance of risk in rate premiums, dividends or benefits of any kind on account of race … and on request of any person whose application for insurance has been rejected the company must furnish them, in writing, the reasons thereof and state that such rejection was not for any racial cause." State Representative S.A. Stockwell, agreed to introduce the bill in the House. The legislature also passed Section 43.5 and 43.24, which forbade discrimination on the basis of religious or political affiliation for any civil service examinations. The necessity of similar legislation in automobile insurance was highlighted in the St. Paul City Council that week, when council members found it necessary to exempt city truck driver Earl Faussett of an insurance requirement because State Farm Mutual of Illinois had dropped him after seven years of accident-free driving on the grounds that, "Negroes do not get fair trials in most courts after they are involved in accidents!"

After the insurance law had been passed in the legislature, Mitchell and Newman met with representatives from Anchor Casualty, the Secretary-Treasurer of the Insurance Federation of Minnesota and Employers Mutual Liability to begin to develop strategies to meet other problems of discrimination in auto insurance. All parties admitted there had been discrimination in the past and the group agreed to drop any color bars they had on liability risk and would undertake personal investigations of complaints of bias.

The most widely discussed civil rights event of 1939 was the denial by the Daughters of the American Revolution (DAR) the right of America's outstanding African-American contralto, Marian Anderson, to perform in the Capital's Constitution Hall. The Minnesota chapter voted 39–1 in support of the national action. Mrs. Eleanor Roosevelt resigned her membership in response to their actions and NAACP Executive Secretary Walter White arranged for Miss Anderson to give her Easter concert on the steps of the Lincoln Memorial which was a huge success attended by over 75,000 persons. In St. Paul, the DAR chapter that had been teaching African-American youngsters a course on "Americanism" at the Hallie Q. Brown Community House were asked to leave the premises by its director, Myrtle Carden, who eliminated the course and noted publicly that "she had grave reservations about the patriotism of any organization which would bar an outstanding American artist from performing in their public facility because of her race."[32]

Early in May, Urban League Executive Secretary, Clarence Mitchell exacted a promise from the St. Paul's Minnesota Milk Company to hire their first African-American driver. The company did not, however, mention to Mitchell that George Holland would be required to sign up 36 customers and have 50 more pledged to accept deliveries after the

15th as the price for his employment. He was also permitted to join Milk Drivers Union #717.[33]

Also that month, the waiters from Local #516 in St. Paul were finally able to persuade the National Mediation Board to require the Great Northern Railway to hold a collective bargaining election on May 22, and the union won by a vote of 113 to 30 over the Great Northern Benefit Association.[33]

Newman also featured Mrs. Frances Pierre Lewis on the front page of the *Recorder* that month, as she observed her 24th anniversary as a prisoner-friend at Stillwater Prison and was presented a large cake by Warden L.F. Utecht.

In June, NAACP chairman John Culver called for a Grand Jury investigation of the death of Thomas "Luckie" Johnson, who had died from an unprovoked attack at the hands of Edward O. Schmidt and Ernest Lukes who had fractured his skull on the evening of September twelfth at Seventh and Wacouta Streets. The Grand Jury was finally called, on October 9th, with S.E. Hall as a member. It indicted the two for manslaughter.[34]

In November, Jane Bolin became the first African-American female judge in the country's history, when she was appointed by Mayor Fiorello La Guardia to be the Judge of the Court of Domestic Relations in New York City.

As the decade drew to a close, Newman had firmly established himself in the eyes of the Twin City African-American community in a role reminiscent of J.Q. Adams. Both were vigilant and relentless fighters for civil and human rights. While Adams occasionally resorted to metaphor to make his points, Newman was more direct and sometimes caustic. Though Adams was a Republican and Newman a Democrat, their party affiliations never stood in the way of putting the interests of their community first. Both kept informed about not only local and state matters, which affected persons of their community but also national news.

Both were educators of the African-American community as well as mentors, advocates and activists. One of the major differences in the circulation of their respective papers was that Newman intended to sell his newspapers to both African-American and white readers with the clear intent to influence both groups in order to improve race relations. He noted that when he started publishing, some whites did not know that there was a racial problem in the Twin Cities. African-Americans were fairly well isolated and had little contact with whites except through domestic or custodial contacts. He noted that most stores did not hire African-Americans as clerks though hotels and clubs did hire them as waiters and cooks. Newman's philosophy was that segregation restricted not only African-Americans but also whites. When Newman expressed these sentiments in his columns, some of his readers failed to understand him and found him too accommodating. He said, "Some have taken to calling me an Uncle Tom, but I am definitely not that." Earlier, he had published a poem depicting the dual countenance African-Americans are often forced to assume in a racist society:

SMILES

There are our smiles of courtesy, diplomacy, approbation and our professional smile,
There are our smiles of pleasure, love, friendship and affection,
There are our smiles of the sweet trusting guileless soul and our complacent smiles of peace, contentment and our hope of a glorified life,
Then there are our disarming smiles of intrigue and betrayal as well as the cynical smiles of our disgust with merely tolerance,
Finally there are our smiles of just plain weariness and resignation which often merely cover our feelings of anger and hate toward the white society.

During the decade of the 30s, Newman felt that African-Americans were merely tolerated as long as they "stayed out of the better eating places" and he remembered when he had arrived in Minneapolis, in 1922, and entered a hamburger shop. He had been very hungry and after he had been served he had taken a large bite only to find that a heavy layer of salt covered the meat. He later told his friends that he, "had smiled and played the part of innocence to perfection but he knew the small quiet Negro in him would never come back again."[35]

CHAPTER SIX BIBLIOGRAPHY

1. *Northwest Monitor*, 30 January 1930.

2. *Northwest Monitor*, 8 July 1930.

3. "Enter the New Negro," *Survey Magazine*, March 1930, pp. 631-636.

4. *Northwest Monitor*, 8 July 1930.

5. *Northwest Monitor*, 23 December 1930.

6. *Northwest Monitor*, 27 January 1931.

7. *Northwest Monitor*, 3 February 1931.

8. *Twin City Herald*, 18 June 1931.

9. *Twin City Herald*, 10 December 1932.

10. *Twin City Herald*, 17 June 1933.

11. *Twin City Herald*, 26 August 1933.

12. *Twin City Herald*, 13 January 1934.

13. *Twin City Herald*, 10 March 1934.

14. *Twin City Herald*, 28 April 1934.

15. Leopold, L.E., *Cecil E. Newman: Newspaper Publisher*, T.S. Denison & Company, Minneapolis, 1969. P. 89.

16. *St. Paul Recorder*, 25 October 1935.

17. *St. Paul Recorder*, 3 April 1936.

18. *St. Paul Recorder*, 9 June 1936.

19. *St. Paul Recorder*, 10 July 1936.

20. *St. Paul Recorder*, 26 February 1937.

21. *St. Paul Recorder*, 12 March 1937.

22. *St. Paul Recorder*, 2 April 1937.

23. See References Below

24. *St. Paul Recorder*, 29 June 1937.

25. See References Below

26. See References Below

27. See References Below

28. See References Below

29. *St. Paul Recorder*, 6 May 1938.

30. See References Below

31. Griffin, James, B*lacks in the St. Paul Fire Department: 1885-1976*, E. and J. Publishers, St. Paul, MN. 1976. p. 36.

32. *St. Paul Recorder*, 13 April 1939.

33. See References Below

34. See References Below

35. See References Below

Additional References:

As a result of the reconstruction of this manuscript several references may have come from these sources below.

a.   Ryder, Walter S., "The Negro in St. Paul," *Opportunity Magazine*, June 1930, pp.170-173.

b.   Walters, Ronald W., *Black Presidential Politics in America*, University of New York Press, 1988, p.17.

c.   Bergam, Peter M., *The Chronological History of the Negro in America*, Harper and Rowe Publishers, New York, pp.463-486.

d.   *St. Paul Recorder*, 2 October 1934.

e.   *St. Paul Recorder*, 4 February 1937.

f.   *Twin City Leader*, 21 December 1940.

g. McWatt, Arthur C., "What's Historic About This Site?" *Ramsey County History Magazine*, Spring 1993.

h. Rose, Robert, *Lonely Eagles: The Story of America's Black Air Force in World War II*, Tuskegee Airmen Inc., Los Angeles, CA, 1980, p.15.

Chapter Seven
1940 – 1949

"We must realize that our future lies chiefly in our own hands. We know that neither institutions nor friends can make a race stand unless it has strength in its own foundations; that races, like individuals must stand or fall by their own merit; that to fully succeed they must practice the virtues of self-reliance, self-respect, industry, perseverance and economy."

Paul Robeson

On January 26, 1940, the entire African-American delegation at the Labor Progressive convention in St. Paul, voted against endorsing John B. "Johnny" Mauer as a candidate for the St. Paul City Council because of his declared policy of discouraging African-American trade in his bar. Among those voting against him were Reginald Harris, John Walton and Maceo Littlejohn. Mauer still managed to win the endorsement by one vote.

During the same week, architectural designer Clarence Wesley Wigington who was America's first African-American architect employed by a municipal government was chosen chief designer of the St. Paul Winter Carnival's Ice Palace. One of its features was a postal station where carnival goers could mail packages.

Wigington had moved to St. Paul in 1915, after having studied under Thomas R. Kimball, who at the time was president of the American Institute of Architects. He had also studied two years under Elfred Turgni, six years under Thomas Kilgohart and one year under Gordon Van Dyne, of Davenport, Iowa. The Department of Parks, Playgrounds and Public Buildings hired him in St. Paul as an architectural draftsman. During his 27-year tenure with the department, Wigington designed the ever-imposing Highland Water Tower, which dominates the city's western skyline. While on a leave of absence during the 1920s, he designed St. James A.M.E. Church.[1] His other designs included Marshall, Wilson, and Monroe High Schools, Cleveland Junior High as well as Randolph Heights and Como Elementary Schools. In 1938, he designed both Holman Airport's administration building and the Keller Golf Clubhouse. Three years later he designed the Harriet Island Pavilion. After being regularly passed over for the post of City Architect for over two decades, Wigington left St. Paul in the early 1940s, but not before the St. Paul Sterling Club honored him, "for giving the community twenty-five years of distinguished service to the field of architecture."[2]

Also in January, African-American citizens began to complain to Editor Newman that the Stassen administration was sending all their African-American Civilian Conservation Corps (CCC) youngsters to the South whereas the previous Benson administration had tried to keep most of them in Minnesota. Jonas Schwartz, Irving Blumber and Sam Scheiner also condemned the governor for his refusal, while serving as the commander-in-chief, of the State National Guard, to allow African-Americans to join the Minnesota Home Defense Force.

Minnesota's African-Americans were pleased the following month to see that the U.S. Post Office had issued a stamp with the likeness of Booker T. Washington, which was the first stamp ever issued in honor of an African-American man by the department. That month the St. Paul Urban League also reported that during the past year they had been successful in finding employment for African-American clients at the Minnesota Mild Company, Schunemans Department Store, Schmidt's Brewery, the Twin City Rapid Transit Company, the Ford Motor Company, the Golden Rule, Field Schlicks, and the Lowry Hotel. The League had added at least $35,000 in wages to St. Paul's African-American community. In addition, Bert Shannon became a driver for Tasty Bakery, but as was the case with George Holland, he was required to obtain a customer quota before his appointment was confirmed.[3]

In March, Louis Ervin contended that the Census Bureau should hire at least 10 African-American enumerators of the 300 allowed to St. Paul, based on the 1940 census. Mr. Willard Moran, of the bureau, however, declared that enumerators were being awarded for every 1,400 persons in the population and on that basis the St. Paul African-American community would receive only 3 for their 4,001 persons of the city's current population.[4]

In July, the Golden Rule Department Store displayed a grotesque caricature of an African-American woman picking cotton, in celebration of National Cotton Week. Mrs. William Godette voiced her disapproval to the store's management and the offending figurine was removed. A letter to Mrs. Godette was sent by the store's manager to express his regret and told her that no offense had been intended.[5]

That summer, after 13 African-American mess men serving on the Navy cruiser Philadelphia signed a letter to the Pittsburgh Courier describing themselves as, "sea-going bellhops, chambermaids and dishwashers." The Navy retaliated by discharging the entire baker's dozen as undesirables and Secretary of the Navy William Franklin "Frank" Knox defended the policy by noting the impossibility of other assignments, because of the close living conditions required aboard ship.[6]

On August 22, Hamlet B. "Kid" Rowe, a sports writer for the *Twin City Herald*, who had been instrumental in bringing interracial boxing to St. Paul, died. Near the end of the month, editor, J.E. Perry, of the *Twin City Leader* pleaded for his readers to write letters in support of the Geyer Anti-Poll Tax Bill which he contended kept four million African-American people in the South from voting as well as disfranchising 60 percent of the region's poor whites.[7]

Two weeks before the 1940 federal elections, F.D.R. promoted Colonel Benjamin O. Davis, Sr. to the rank of Brigadier General, which undoubtedly helped to win over some African-American voters.

In December, Ben Perry, who criticized the St. Paul YMCA for its policy of restricted swimming for African-American youth was denounced by the agency's director and called a "communist agitator." The director told him the "problem" had been settled two years ago, when the YMCA on Tenth and Cedar had permitted African-American youngsters to swim on Wednesday nights. Perry's response was that, "This won't be settled until I can go swimming whichever day I want."[8]

In 1940, for the first time in the 20th century, the Democratic National platform mentioned the word Negro and pledged to uphold "due process (the Fifth Amendment) and equal protection (the Fourteenth Amendment) of the U.S. Constitution for every citizen regardless of race, creed or color." In the national election, however, the Democratic Party's "New Deal" which promised to end discrimination in relief agencies and defense industries received only 40 percent of the African-American vote.[9]

On January 25, 1941, Under-Secretary of War Robert T. Patterson announced that a "Negro" air squadron of 27 planes and 33 officer-pilots as well as a ground crew of 407 was being organized by the U.S. Army Air Force. The group would be assembled at Chanute Field, Illinois, for pre-flight training before going to Tuskegee, Alabama, for flight-training. The first flying cadets were inducted into the Army flying school and began their primary training on July 19, 1941. Twelve cadets and one student officer reported for pre-flight training. The student-officer was 1936 West Point graduate, Captain Benjamin O. Davis, Jr. At the time he and his father General B.O. Davis, Sr. were the only two African-American line-officers in the U.S. Army. Captain Davis completed his flight training and became the first African-American man to officially solo an aircraft as an officer of the U.S. Army Air Corps on September 2, 1941.[10]

In February, the Minnesota Defense Force continued to refuse African-American applications according to Sam Reed, who headed the St. Paul legal defense committee. Governor Stassen also refused to meet with the committee and Lee Turpin threatened to bring an injunction against the governor to force him to carry out his duties as Commander of the State Defense Force and admit him to membership. Attorney R.A. Skinner volunteered to bring the suit. Unfortunately, Turpin was drafted before the suit could be filed.

Later in the month, some dissident St. Paul Democrats facetiously invited Representative Theodore Bilbo of Mississippi to speak on March 29th at their Jefferson-Jackson Day dinner on his "Back to Africa" bill.[11]

That April, the efforts of William H. Gaston, a retired St. Paul police officer, were rewarded when Representative John Drexler of the State Legislature finally introduced his bill. The bill was reported out of the labor committee and was passed with a comfortable majority. It prohibited discrimination in employment contracts of state, county, city, town and school districts (Section 181.59). It was signed into law by Governor Stassen on April 16th.[12]

Also in May, the U.S. Supreme Court ruled that, "Negroes must be furnished accommodations by railroads as good as those furnished whites."[13] This occurred after the Court heard a suit brought by the country's sole African-American U.S. Representative, Arthur Mitchell, who had been forced from a Pullman sleeper, in Arkansas, four years earlier. By the end of month, the St. Paul Urban League was successful in getting Willard Moore hired as a furniture salesman at Cardozos Furniture Store.

In June, BSCP leader Frank Boyd was named chairman of the, "On to Washington," NAACP steering committee and he named Mrs. Carrie McWatt, of the Ladies Auxiliary as a member. The march, scheduled for July 1st, was postponed to June 25th, when President Roosevelt issued Executive Order 8802 after a conferring with A. Philip Randolph, Walter White and Aubrey Williams. His order forbade racial discrimination by defense employers and trade unionists. The order set up a five-man Fair Employment Practices Committee (FEPC) to investigate and to act upon complaints of discrimination.

In September, the state convention of the Congress of Industrial Organizations (CIO) went on record as being unilaterally opposed to discrimination in both the state and nation and denounced segregation in both the army and the navy. Copies of their resolution were sent to the President, the Secretary of War, and Navy and the Minnesota Defense Board. The state American Federation of Labor (AFL) tried to pass a similar proposal at their convention, but it was pointed out that 22 of its affiliates still have constitutional bars against African-American members.[14]

The war provided African-American Minnesotans new job opportunities under Executive Order 8802. Not only were they involved in the building of Charles Lilley Horn's Federal Cartridge Corporation, in New Brighton, but beginning that October, 2500 African-American applicants were screened for plant employment. Cecil Newman, who always referred to Horn as his "first subscriber," was hired as Horn's Administrative Assistant. Under his guidance, and with the support of both Twin City Urban Leagues, over 2,000 African-American workers were assigned to 41 different job categories.[15]

During this same period Newman signed up to serve in the Minnesota Home Militia but was rejected by the Governor who claimed he had no power to integrate it. After a considerable number of protests and editorials, Stassen appointed Sam Ransom as a lone African-American Major to the Minnesota National Guard, which undermined Newman's campaign for integration. However, he diminished the governor's actions when he pointed out in an editorial that "Major Ransom was a commander without troops."[16]

In 1942, S. Vincent Owens became the Executive Secretary of the St. Paul Urban League. Owens was born in Missouri and received his early education in Salinas, Kansas, and after finishing high school, he enrolled at the University of Kansas where he earned a B.S. degree in sociology. After college, he married his fiancé, Wanda, and held a variety of jobs including work on the railroad as a waiter before joining the League. Owen's first office was located in downtown St. Paul, on the corner of Cedar and Sixth Streets. During that year, Owens assigned Charles Rogers, his newly appointed Industrial Secretary, the task of doing a state survey on African-American employment, which was subsequently published by the newly formed Governor's Interracial Commission the following year.

That April, Mr. Owens and Wallace Robinson, the President of the St. Paul Urban League, were called to mediate a walk out of workers at the Star Laundry. The walk out occurred after a Miss Dorothy Brown, an African-American sorter, had been hired. During a conference called by Mr. Fink, the owner, the head sorter, Owens, was told that the other workers objected to Miss Brown, because, "Negroes had an offensive odor due to the color of their skin." Mr. Owens, told her that all work-ers have offensive odors if they failed to wash and though they were objecting to working with African-Americans, a large part of the clothes they were handling came from African-American patrons. The matter was resolved when Mr. Fink told them that if any more walked off the job because of Miss Brown, they would not be permitted to return.[17]

That summer Owens succeeded in placing Miss DeVaughnia Coleman at International Harvester as a machine operator, which was the first time an African-American had ever been employed at the Midway facility. In July, Owens announced the hiring of two power machine operators by the B.W. Harris Manufacturing Company. Mrs. William Nathan and Mrs. Verna Hickman welcomed both operators, to membership in the CIO's Amalgamated Clothing Workers of America.

That fall, Clarence Mitchell visited St. Paul and toured the American Hoist and Derrick Company and Minnesota Mining and Manufacturing (3M), both of who had formerly discriminated against African-American applicants when Mitchell had been with the League.

Mitchell, was now the Assistant Director of the War Manpower Commission and less than a week after his visit, the American Hoist and Derrick Company hired African-Americans Thomas Pater and James E. Howard as laborers and before the visit ended, 3M told Owens that they would be accepting applications of African-American workers between the ages of 20 and 40 years of age.[18]

At year's end, Asa Philip Randolph was awarded the Spingarn Medal by the NAACP for his, "fearless and determined mobilization of mass opinion which resulted in the signing of Executive Order 8802."[19]

In January 1943, former St. Paul civil rights activists and then Regimental Sergeant Major Sam Reed was demoted at Camp Lee, Virginia. Reed had been serving as the chairman of a committee who presented grievances to his commanding officer, Colonel Henry, about the poor treatment of African-American soldiers. Colonel Henry, in turn, accused Reed of "destroying an order which included an application of a private for officers candidate school." Walter White, who was an investigator for the NAACP said the charges were false and he intended to place the matter before the House Military Affairs Committee. In the meantime, Reed was shipped over-seas without rank to North Africa.[20]

In February, after a Jewish soldier was refused service in a St. Paul tavern, the Minnesota Civil Rights Law (Section 327.09), which forbade discrimination in public places on the basis of race, creed or color was extended to include, "national origins." Later in that month, S. Vincent Owens led a group of St. Paul citizens to the offices of station KSTP to protest the airing of a program that referred to French Senegalese troops as, "long-legged niggers." Station officials told Owens that it was a part of the company's advertising, which was handled by Batten, Barton, Dursten and Osburn and that they had no control over it. Owens told them a protest would be made to the Federal Communications Commission if the offensive segment was aired again and it was quietly dropped.[21]

In March, U.S. Representative Vito Marcantonio introduced a discharge petition for the Anti-Poll Tax bill he had introduced in the House of Representatives, which he claimed would allow six million poor whites and four million poor blacks to vote in eight southern states.

That spring, Waldorf Paper Products followed the lead of 3M and told the Urban League's Vincent Owens that they now were accepting African-American applicants between the ages of 18 and 45.

In May, Adolph Thomas of 735 St. Anthony became the first African-American in St. Paul to be accepted by the U.S. Marines and join its 33rd Platoon.

During the first week of August, St. Paul's NAACP Legal Redress Chairman, Maceo Littlejohn, convinced Commissioner Fred Truax to redress a discriminatory policy at the Harriet Island Roller Rink, which had refused admittance to Eugene Ross.[22]

The following month, Mr. Owens was able to get Purcell Parker a job on the Alaskan Highway Project. He did it by finding out when he would be taking his discharge physical at Fort Snelling and coordinating it with a job interview and physical with the Alaskan Highway Project. After Purcell had completed his examination at the Fort, Owens drove him directly to the second interview and exam. After completing his written tests, Purcell was given his physical and when he was told that he had failed to pass he called in Owens as his witness and presented the results of his service discharge to the Metcalf Hamilton Construction Company's doctor and was immediately passed. Prior to Parker's acceptance, the contractors for the highway project had consistently turned down all African-American applicants because of failed medical exams. The subterfuge by Owens resulted in additional African-American workers being accepted after Owens had broken the rule.[23]

In November, the Army and Navy announced that they desperately needed 60,000 nurses for the armed services but still refused to increase their quota of 160 African-American nurses that had been set. African-

American women continued to serve in the Army's WACs the Navy's WAVES, the Coast Guard's SPARS and the Air Force's WAFS.[24]

On December 5th, Stanley Harris of the 99th Pursuit Squadron became the first African-American St. Paul airman to win his wings at Tuskegee Institute. He was later promoted to captain and was awarded six Oak Leaf Clusters after being overseas for eleven months.

At the end of the year, the U.S. Supreme Court ruled that the 45 Red Caps who worked in the St. Paul Union Station should have the Brotherhood of Railway Steamship Clerks, Freight Handlers, and Express and Station Employees act as their collective bargaining agent, even though that union denied them membership. Judge James A. Cobb, who represented the CIO's Transport Service Employees who were attempting to gain the right to represent the Red Caps as their bargaining agent compared the court's decision with that of Chief Justice Taney's Dred Scott Decision of 1857. Later the court ruled that Red Caps had to agree to be represented by the Brotherhood of Railway Trainmen who had been largely responsible for the elimination of all African-American engineers and firemen during the early decades of the century.[25]

In February 1944, a major concern to African-American workers were the hearings that were held on Capitol Hill by the Fair Employment Practices Commission, which disclosed that the Brotherhood of Locomotive Engineers and Firemen, with the consent of the Railway Labor Board, had inserted a clause in their constitution which prohibited African-American firemen from ever becoming engineers. Decades earlier, almost all southern railroad firemen had been African-American. The hearings subsequently disclosed that ten of the fourteen major U.S. railroads were continuing to ignore the F.E.P.C.'s orders to hire African-American firemen, train conductors and yard foremen.[26]

In March 1944, the Green-Lucas bill was being debated in the Senate, which would have given active soldiers the right to vote in federal elections. Senator Eastland (D-MS) led a filibuster against it on the grounds, "it would upset the Southern way of life." However, the National Opinion Research Center at the University of Denver reported that they had found that 92 percent of the American population favored it for overseas soldiers and 77 percent favored it for soldiers stationed in the U.S. Shortly after these results were reported in the press, restrictions were lifted on the rights of African-American seamen to only do shore duty and quotas were established in both the Coast Guard and the Marine Corps for African-American applicants. Unfortunately, this good news had to be tempered by the biased remarks of Secretary of War Henry L. Stimson, who when later questioned by Representative Hamilton Fish, as to why more African-American had not been used more in combat, replied, "Unfortunately, many of the Negro units have not been able to master, efficiently the techniques of our modern weapons."[27]

In April, the Democratic Party named labor advocate Frank Boyd a Presidential Elector, while employment advocate S.E. Hall was named one by the Republican Party.

In May, Charles Rogers of the St. Paul Urban League had not only been successful in getting African-Americans admitted as members to the St. Paul YMCA, but had also been helpful in getting Seegar Refrigerator Company, Griggs and Cooper and Brown and Bigelow Advertising Company to agree to employ African-Americans. In the nation's Capital May 17th, the bill was reported out of the House Judiciary Committee, which made it a federal offense to assault a member of the armed forces. The Senate had passed it the previous year as S.R. 1227, but it soon became bogged down in conference committee with Southerners seeing to it that it was never reported out. It later became a lobbying issue and a recruitment ploy for the newly organized American Veterans Committee (AVC).

CRUSADERS FOR JUSTICE

Early in June, Major Sam Ransom won a discrimination suit against the C & O Café at 540 Rice Street for their refusal to serve either himself or his wife on separate occasions. Proprietor Anton Sivitek was fined $100 and was forced to serve six months in the county workhouse.

Also in June, Editor Newman printed a "Credo for the Negro Press" by P. Bernard Young:

> I shall crusade for all things that are right and just and I will, with equal fervor, expose and condemn all things that are unjust.
> I shall be an advocate for the full practice of the principles implicit in the concept of Life, Liberty and Justice for All.
> I shall be an advocate for the human and civil rights on behalf of those to whom they are denied and I shall turn the pitiless light of publicity upon all who would deny those rights to others.
> I shall herald those tidings, good and bad on the faith that the people are free only if the truth is known to them.
> I shall mirror and record, our resistance as it is and all our striving to better our lot
> I shall not only be a crusader, and advocate, a mirror, a record, a herald and a spotlight but I also shall not falter, So Help me God![28]

In the middle of June, Ben Perry became the first African-American Minnesotan to be chosen a delegate to the National Convention of the American Legion, which was being held in Chicago.

In September, the *Recorder* reported 13 million African-Americans in the U.S. had a gross annual income of seven billion dollars of which 42 percent was spent on consumer goods according to David J. Sullivan of the Negro Digest.

The previous year, the annual income of America's African-American population had exceeded the gross national income of Canada by over a billion dollars.[29]

CHAPTER SEVEN 1940 – 1949

Early in October, Walter White, the National Executive Secretary of the NAACP, reported that a Private Spicely had been killed by a Durham, North Carolina bus driver, whom the jury had acquitted in a record time of 28 minutes.[30]

On October 16th, Marie E. "Bessie" Farr, who had been born in St. Paul in 1860, died at the age of 84 on October 16th. She had been the first African-American graduate of Central High School in 1881 and a generation later was appointed to teach second grade at Lincoln Elementary School, which she did for almost a decade.[31]

By the end of the year, three of the most satisfying political events for African-American voters were the election of Adam Clayton Powell Jr. (D-NY) to the Seventy-First Congress, the U.S. Supreme Court decision that white primaries violated the Fifteenth Amendment (Smith v. Allwright) and that persons had a right to work in a closed shop when union membership had been denied them on the grounds of their race or color (James v. Marineship Corporation).

Early in 1945, when Robert S. Johnson offered a course, at the University of Minnesota, on, "Appreciation of the Negro in American History." It caused Editor Newman to reflect in an editorial on the praises, which Minnesotans had recently bestowed on Governor Aides Billy Williams and George Hoage. These two outstanding African American men had served ten governors as appointment aides over a 46-year period and had gained the respect and admiration of all who knew them. Newman bemoaned that fact that such obviously talented and charming men had been forced to serve out their lives in such a minor capacity due to the lack of opportunities offered them because of their color.

After New York passed the Ives-Quinn bill establishing the nation's first Fair Employment Practices Commission (FEPC), S. Vincent Owens began an active lobbying effort to get FEPC legislation enacted in Minnesota. He also announced that he had succeeded in getting

Virginia Kipper, Millicent Marshall and Lucille Burris hired as production workers at the local 3M plant.

In February, U.S. Representative Adam Clayton Powell was able to get his "Powell Amendment," which would stop states who discriminated against African-Americans from receiving federal funds, attached to the $100 million school lunch bill. It passed by a vote of 258–109 for his first national legislative victory.[32]

Though millions of African-Americans were saddened by the death of F.D.R. in April, many were distressed to learn that Mrs. Mary McLeod Bethune had been the only notable African-American invited to attend the funeral service.

In June, Newman chided the African-American parents of Minneapolis high school graduates for having only seven graduates while St. Paul parents had graduated thirty-five. He also noted that most of the Minneapolis youngsters were boys and quoted an African proverb, which said, "When you educate a man you educate an individual, but when you educate a woman, you educate a family."

The following month Congress ignored the pleas of Senator Wayne Morse (R-OR) to strengthen the federal FEPC and instead cut its budget to $250,000 and slashed the agency's staff from 117 to 51. Only a parliamentary move by Representative Vito Anthony Marcantonio, American Labor Party – New York, saved the bill from being killed.[33]

When William Herron, a Twin City labor organizer, attended the CIO convention in July, he was refused accommodations at the Ambassador Hotel in the nation's capitol. Instead of accepting it meekly, Herron immediately contacted the hotel's union steward and convinced him to shut down the hotel. Hotel management panicked and for the rest of his stay, Herron said he was treated like royalty by the entire hotel staff.

CHAPTER SEVEN 1940 – 1949

As the war drew to a close, it was discovered that the 332nd had flown more combat missions (1,578) than any other group in Europe, as well as 15,000 sorties. 450 graduates of the Tuskegee program flew combat missions, 65 were killed in action, and 23 were shot down and became prisoners of war. The official accounts list 136 enemy aircraft destroyed or damaged in the air and another 273 destroyed on the ground. The one statistic that stands above all other is a zero for the number of escorted Allied bombers lost to enemy fighters.[34]

The war record of the Tuskegee airmen was further enhanced at the All-Air Force National Flying and Gunnery competition at Las Vegas, where Captain Alva Temple, Lt. James Harvey, Lt. Harry Steward and Lt. Halbert Alexander beat all competition in air gunnery, rocket firing, strafing, dive bombing and skip bombing.[35]

That summer, Newman made one of his most enduring and satisfying friendships of his life when he gave his support to Hubert Humphrey, who was running for Mayor of Minneapolis. His *Spokesman* was the only newspaper in the city that supported Humphrey's campaign and though he lost the election he never forgot Newman's loyalty. When he ran two years later and won he established a City Human Relations Council at Newman's request.

At the end of the year, the Governor's Interracial Commission released a report from 601 of the 2,231 questionnaires that had been sent to Twin City employers. From those returned, only 117 had said that they presently employed African-Americans while another 321 said they would not employ them. Of the 54,334 union members only 646 were African-American. One of the things that was encouraging was that of the 109 unions that responded, 104 of them said that they favored accepting African-Americans for full membership. After reading the report, Governor Luther Youngdahl, commenting on it said that, "Whenever any member of our society finds the door of opportunity closed because of the color of their skin or the nature of their religious faith, democracy suffers a tragic defeat and the fate of us all becomes a little less secure."[36]

In May 1946, the St. Paul NAACP found it necessary to come to the defense of the world-famous Southernaires singing group who had been told by the St. Paul Hotel desk clerk that their reservation had "disappeared." When that matter was finally settled they had to, almost immediately, aid NAACP field representatives Reverend Raymond Lockridge and Mrs. Jessie Dedmen, who had come to investigate the matter and had also been turned away without explanation.[37]

Later that spring, at an NAACP rally which brought army veteran, Isaac Woodward and his sister to the Hallie Q. Brown Community House to raise money for an appeal against the unprovoked brutality that he had endured in Aikon, Georgia. Woodward was a 27-year-old African-American soldier who had served five years in the armed services. When he was given his discharge he returned to his hometown. When he failed to move fast enough in getting off a local bus he was pulled off by Sheriff Lyndwood Shull who gouged both his eyes with the end of his night stick. When Woodward's sister sought treatment for him at a local veteran's hospital, it was denied because the wounds were not "service connected." When she applied for disability payments they told her they were not available to her because she had not been listed as a "dependent" which is the same reason Nellie Francis was denied her husband's death benefits a generation earlier. U.S. Attorney General Tom Clark filed criminal charges against Shull for violating Woodward's civil rights, but an Aikon jury took only fifteen minutes to find their sheriff not guilty.[38]

Two years earlier, Irene Morgan of Gloucester, Virginia, had boarded a bus for Baltimore and had refused the driver's demand to give up her seat to a white man and was fined $10. On June 3, 1946, the case was argued before the Supreme Court by Thurgood Marshall, who not only succeeded in having her conviction overturned but also was awarded a ruling that segregation on interstate buses was illegal.[39]

In August, Solomon Hughes, a Minneapolis golfer, and Ted Rhodes, one of the nation's leading African-American golfers, were both denied entry to St. Paul's 14th Annual Open Golf Tournament. When Vincent Owens attempted to publish that fact, Ben Ridder, publisher of the *St. Paul Dispatch* and *Pioneer Press*, refused to run it on the grounds that it would "only antagonize the PGA."[40]

In September, St. Paul's Dorie Miller, Post 554 of the American Legion, sponsored a resolution that they sent to their national executive committee urging the Legion to work to end the poll tax in all states of the Union.

In November, a significant civil rights gain was made in St. Paul when Dr. Paul Dwan of the University of Minnesota's School of Medicine announced at a press conference that blood plasma at the University would no longer be segregated in the state's blood bank that he supervised for the American Red Cross.[41]

The following month, Paul Bremeicker, the Executive-Secretary of the St. Paul YMCA, announced another break-through when he told the Methodist Preachers Association that his organization was dropping all racial barriers for accommodations in addition to memberships and all African-American patrons would be accorded equal treatment.

These gains were due at least in part to the efforts of the newly organized St. Paul Council of Human Relations which had recently elected the Reverend Philip McNairy as its first president. The organization was one of the first of its kind in the nation and its board included the Reverend Benjamin Moore, of Pilgrim Baptist Church, Mrs. Samuel Reed, and S. Vincent Owens. The council had developed programs of sensitivity-training for police officers, inter-cultural programs for public school teachers and a legal-assistance branch headed by Warren Burger. The *Recorder* had praised Burger earlier in the year for his brilliant court summation, which overturned Judge Round's recommendations to the jury concerning Nelson Perry's alleged misconduct on the campus of St. Paul's Concordia College.

The year ended with the Spingarn Medal being presented to Thurgood Marshall, the director of the NAACP's Legal Defense and Educational Fund, "for his distinguished service as a lawyer before the Supreme Court."

In January 1947, Editor Newman lauded the contributions of music and drama critic, John Harvey, of the St. Paul Pioneer-Press who for many years had never missed an opportunity to give favorable mention or praise for the accomplishments of African-American artists or to any program devoted to the welfare of minorities.

Later in the month, John Hickman, the son of pioneer Robert Hickman, died. He had been the first Minnesota-born student of color to graduate from a Minnesota Law School. He had graduated, in 1907, at the age 22 from the St. Paul College of Law. After graduation; however, he was unable to make a living from his legal fees, for himself or his family and was forced to seek other employment, which he did at the St. Paul Post Office where he worked for the next 44 years.

Later in January, Arthur Sternberg, an attorney with the St. Paul NAACP, Dr. M.A. Morrel, the Dean of Hamline University and the Reverend T. R. Nelson, of Camphor Methodist Church, staged a 12 hour sit-in, from 8 p.m. to 8 a.m., in the lobby of the Hamline Hotel. This was done because of the management's refusal to accept the reservation of CORE's Secretary Treasurer, Bayard Rustin. The following morning, management finally agreed to accept Rustin and he later reported that he was treated well for the remainder of his stay.[42]

In February, Charles Rogers, the Industrial Secretary of the St. Paul Urban League, was successful in getting Alfred Stewart employed as the city's second African American streetcar motorman.

Early that summer, Carl Ward and Bob Sutton, of WCCO produced a radio show entitled, "Neither Free Nor Equal." The program had been developed by Sig Nickleson, the station's Director for News and Special Events, and much of the material had been provided by the Governor's Interracial Commission, the St. Paul Council on Human Relations, and the Minneapolis Mayor's Council on Human Relations. The following year the program was presented the Outstanding Achievement Award from the National Council of Christians and Jews.

About this time, Detective Paul Hanft of the St. Paul Council of Human Relations, convinced the group to being the distributors of a pamphlet called, "Outside the Home." The pamphlet was sent to each newly licensed proprietor, and every policeman, and hotel manager. They helped to explain Minnesota's civil rights laws and urged them to inform their fellow employees and workers to please observe them.

Later that summer, Major Sam Ransom, also chaired a meeting to chart a course for opening up the Minnesota National Guard to African-American enlistees. Earlier that spring he had resigned his commission in protest to the existing policy. At the meeting were LaPercelle Greene, who was commander of the Twin City Veterans of Foreign Wars, Byron Riffe, who was the commander of the American Legion's Dorie Miller Post, Stephen Maxwell, the commander of the Legion's Attucks-Brooks Post, Jim Lee, the commander of the Leslie Lawrence Post and Charles Smith, who commanded the Johnny Baker Post. Their proposals were sent to Governor Luther Youngdahl, who appointed Father Gilligan of the Interracial Commission as mediator with the Guard in the hopes of reaching a solution.

Late in the summer, the Governor's Interracial Commission reported at their annual dinner that 47 percent of the Negro families in St. Paul owned their own homes compared to 51 percent of whites. They also disclosed that 62 percent were single-family homes and 68 percent had central heating. The down side was that 50 percent were in segregated neighborhoods and that 20 percent of the homes surveyed were in need of major repairs.[43]

Father Gilligan, who since 1943 had practically run the Commission by himself, asked the board for help and was given the assistance of Clifford Rucker, who was named an Informational Representative to assist him. During the year, the Commission had been instrumental in getting a law passed that banned discrimination on the basis of religion and politics in the selection of tenants for public housing projects (Section 462.481). It had also helped pass a law forbidding discrimination in the use of any land in a redevelopment project (Section 462.525).

Whitney Young

That fall, Miss Olga Anderson became a substitute teacher in St. Paul, and Charles Rogers, who worked for the Urban League for five years, received a contract to teach at Maxfield School. Both joined Miss Rachel James, who was then at Mechanic Arts to make up the African-American teaching cadre in the city.

Whitney Young took over for Rogers at the League. Young was born in Lincoln Ridge, Kentucky and received his early schooling there. He went on to graduate from Kentucky State University before coming to the Twin Cities to attend the University of Minnesota Graduate School of Social Work and received his M.S. in 1947. Later in the year, he became a member of the Minneapolis Junior Chamber of Commerce.

At the end of the year, the Southern Regional Council released figures that only 12 percent of African-Americans in the 12 states of the Deep South met current voting qualifications and in the states of Louisiana, Alabama and Mississippi only 3 percent of African-Americans were qualified which made only 600,000 African-American voters in the entire region eligible. However, with the help of the Political Action Committee of the CIO's Tobacco Workers, the first African-American since Reconstruction was elected to the city council in Winston Salem, North Carolina.[44]

African-Americans throughout the country also rejoiced when Jackie Robinson broke the color-bar in major league baseball to play first base for Branch Rickey's Brooklyn Dodgers. Robinson went on to become the combined leagues' "Rookie of the Year," and also played in the 1947 World Series.

In May, Roy "Campy" Companella, became a catcher for the St. Paul Saints and was the first African-American baseball player ever hired by an American Association team. The Brooklyn Dodgers had bought his contract from Nassau in 1946, and used him on their Montreal team for a short time before sending him to St. Paul.

In June, Anna Arnold, an Iowa-born woman who, in 1922, had been the first African-American graduate of Hamline University, Minnesota's oldest institution of higher learning, received an honorary degree at their graduation ceremonies. Miss Arnold, who grew up in Anoka, after graduation from Hamline, had attempted to find employment practice teaching in St. Paul only to find that the school system would not accept her as a practice teacher. She accepted an offer to teach at Rust College in Holly Springs, Mississippi, for two years before receiving an offer to serve as a YMCA, director in New York City where she served at several urban branches. In 1940, she was the co-sponsor, along with A. Philip Randolph, of the proposed March-on-Washington. She later became the city's first consultant on Racial Problems for a Permanent Fair Employment Practices Commission (FEPC) in 1943 where she developed a national legislative and educational program during the next three years. In 1946, she was appointed assistant dean of women at Howard University.

At the Democratic convention in Philadelphia, on July 14th, Mayor Hubert Humphrey told his fellow delegates, "There are those who say to you—we are rushing the issue of civil rights. I say we are 172 years late. There are those who say—the issue of civil rights is an infringement on states rights. The time has arrived for the Democratic Party to get out of the shadow of states rights and walk forthrightly into the bright sunshine of human rights!" As a result of his remarks, 35 delegates from southern states walked out of the Democratic convention to support Senator Strom Thurmond as their State's Rights Party candidate.

On July 26th, 1940 President Truman was persuaded by the joint efforts of Arnold and Randolph, who had threatened to urge civil disobedience against the draft, to issue Executive Order No. 9981 which directed the U.S. armed forces to give "equality of treatment and opportunity" to ethnics of color.[45]

On the eve of the November elections, President Truman integrated the Great Lakes Naval Training Center. A week later he won the Presidency with the help of 3.5 million African-American votes, while Thurmond carried the Solid South - eleven former Confederate states.

At the state Democratic Convention in Brainerd, Edward Harris, an assistant director of the Brooks Funeral Home in St. Paul, was chosen a Presidential Elector by the largest vote cast at the convention.

The year ended with a major employment break-through in St. Paul, engineered by S. Vincent Owens, which resulted in eight stores hiring a total of fourteen African-American salespersons with Northwestern Bell hiring both Mrs. Josephine Oden and Miss Yvonne Weber as telephone operators.

In January 1949, the national NAACP presented an award of merit to Federal Judge J. Waties Waring, of South Carolina, for restraining state officials from barring African-Americans who wished to vote and another to Dr. Lewis Webster Jones, of the University of Arkansas, for being the first president of a southern medical school to admit African-American students.

The following month, President Truman appointed Mrs. Anna Arnold Hedgeman as an administrative assistant to Federal Security Director, Oscar Ewing, which gave her the highest position then being held by a African-American woman in government.

In March, the Minnesota Junior Chamber of Commerce Poll named Newman one of Minnesota's "100 Living Greats." Soon after receiving it, Newman recommended that his readers fill in the word, "human" on their driver license applications where it asks for their race.

In July, Mrs. Ossie Miller and Mrs. Stella Price, who were delegates to the International Toastmistress convention, were denied accommodations at the St. Paul Hotel for over three hours before a room was finally made available for their use.[46]

In August, NAACP National Director, Walter White named former St. Paul Executive Director Clarence Mitchell as Director of their Washington D.C. Bureau. He became their chief lobbyist for the next two decades.

Also that month, at the state convention of Minnesota's American Legion Chapters 40 and 8, a resolution was offered by St. Paul's Martin Weddington, which asked that the words, "Male and White" be stricken from the national organization's constitution and after its passage it was forwarded to the Legion's national headquarters.

In October, pioneer resident Mrs. William B. Tady was asked by the operators of the Bethesda Invalid Home, at 9th and Wacouta, to leave, "because we have never had Negroes before." Fortunately, Mrs. Tady was subsequently admitted to the Quinlan Nursing Home at 23 West Fifth Street.[47]

In late November, Truman chose William Hastie to become the first African-American to sit on a U.S. Court of Appeals while Representative

William L. Dawson (D-Il) became the first African-American Congressman to head a standing committee of the Congress.

Just before the Christmas break, the St. Paul Urban League Industrial Secretary, Whitney Young, with Arthur McWatt visited fraternity and sorority houses on the University of Minnesota campus to speak out against discriminatory clauses in their fraternity constitutions and to ask their help in eliminating them. Young and McWatt were able to convince three of them to drop their discriminatory clauses that year.[48]

As the decade drew to a close it was obvious that Roosevelt's New Deal had given the nation's African-American citizens renewed hope and fresh opportunities from an economy that was becoming increasingly committed to defense. The crisis was helping the nation pull itself out of its economic doldrums.

In the Twin Cities, the Urban Leagues had expanded its job offerings from less than a dozen job categories for African-American workers to over one hundred with Twin City Federal Cartridge Corporation and other defense contractors being major contributors.

During the latter half of the decade the G.I. Bill offered education and job training to those returning veterans of color, of whom many began to accept the inevitability of their condition in the following verse.

> How Come?
> When I was born I was black,
> When I grew up I was black,
> When I am sick I am black,
> When I go out into the sun I am black,
> When I die I will be black,
> But You;
> When you were born you were pink,
> When you grow up you will be white,
> When you get very sick you will be green,

CHAPTER SEVEN 1940 – 1949

When you go out in the sun you will be red,
When you die you will be purple,
So, Please, just call me Black!

CHAPTER SEVEN BIBLIOGRAPHY

1. McWatt, Arthur C., "What's Historic About This Site?" *Ramsey County History*, Spring 1993.

2. *St. Paul Recorder*, 26 January 1940.

3. *St. Paul Recorder*, 12 February 1940.

4. *St. Paul Recorder*, 29 March 1940.

5. *St. Paul Recorder*, 19 July 1940.

6. Astor, Gerald, *The Right to Fight*, Presido Press, Vocato, California, 1998, p. 159.

7. *Twin City Leader*, 31 August 1940.

8. *Twin City Leader*, 21 December 1940.

9. Bergman, Peter M. *The Negro in America; The Chronological History*, Harpers and Row, New York, 1969, pp. 491–2.

10. Rose, Robert A. D.D.S., *Lonely Eagles: The Story of America's Black Air Force in World War II*, Tuskegee Airman Inc., 1976, Los Angeles, p. 12-15.

11. *St. Paul Recorder*, 28 March 1941.

12. *St. Paul Recorder*, 11 April 1941.

13. *St. Paul Recorder*, 2 May 1941.

14. *St. Paul Recorder*, 12 September 1941.

15. Leipold L.E. *Cecil Newman: Newspaper Publisher*, pp. 97–98.

16. ibid.. p. 104.

17. *St. Paul Recorder*, 10 April 1942.

18. *St. Paul Recorder*, 23 October 1942.

19. *St. Paul Recorder*, 4 December 1942.

20. *St. Paul Recorder*, 15 January 1943.

21. *St. Paul Recorder*, 12 February 1943.

22. *St. Paul Recorder*, 6 August 1943.

23. *St. Paul Recorder*, 2 September 1943.

24. *St. Paul Recorder*, 5 November 1943.

25. *St. Paul Recorder*, 17 December 1943.

26. *St. Paul Recorder*, 18 February 1944.

27. *St. Paul Recorder*, 13 March 1944.

28. *St. Paul Recorder*, 30 June 1944.

29. *St. Paul Recorder*, 29 September 1944.

30. *St. Paul Recorder*, 6 October 1944.

31. *St. Paul Recorder*, 20 October 1944.

32. Haygood, Wil, *King of the Cats: The Life and Times of Adam Clayton Powell Jr.*, Houghton Mifflin Company, New York, 1993, p. 134.

33. *St. Paul Recorder*, 20 July 1945.

34. Astor, Gerald, *The Right to Fight*, p. 306.

35. Frances, Charles F., *The Tuskegee Airmen; The Men Who Changed the Nation*, Brandon Publishing Company, Boston, 1988, p. 232.

36. *Report of the Governor's Interracial Commission*, "The Negro Worker," 1945, pp. 7–15.

37. *St. Paul Recorder*, 17 May 1946.

38. *St. Paul Recorder*, 19 July 1946.

39. Williams, Juan, *Thurgood Marshall: American Revolutionary*, Random House, New York City, N.Y., 1996, p. 145

40. *St. Paul Recorder*, 13 August 1946.

41. *St. Paul Recorder*, 8 November 1946.

42. *St. Paul Recorder*, 24 January 1947.

43. *St. Paul Recorder*, 1 August 1947.

44. Bergman, Peter M. *The Negro in America*, p. 514.

45. Anderson, Jervis, *A. Philip Randolph, A Biographical Portrait*, Harcort Brace, New York, 1972, p. 280.

46. *St. Paul Recorder*, 29 July 1949.

47. *St. Paul Recorder*, 14 October 1949.

48. Dickerson, Dennis C. *Militant Mediator: Whitney M. Young Jr.*, The University of Kentucky Press, Lexington, Kentucky, 1998, p. 49.

Chapter Eight
1950 – 1959

"We will not be satisfied to take one jot or title less than our full manhood rights. We claim for ourselves every single right that belongs to a free-born American, political, civil and social; and until we get these rights we will never cease to protest and assail the ears of America with the story of its shameful deeds."

W.E.B. DuBois, Harpers Ferry, NY, 1906

The 1950 U.S. Census found that the 15,042,286 African-Americans in America constituted about 10 percent of the country's population and that African-American male life expectancy was six years less than the 66.5 years of white males. African-American female expectancy was nine years less than their white counterparts. Thirteen percent of the African-American population lived in the northeast, 15 percent in the north central; only 4 percent lived in the West while 68 percent still lived in the South. Fifty-seven percent of whites owned their own homes compared to only 35 percent of African-Americans.[1]

That spring, in St. Paul African-American bowlers Ralph Jones, Ernest Green, Bob Gaines and William McIntosh broke the American Bowling Congress' "all white" rule when they insisted upon entering the Minneapolis Tribune Annual Bowling Classic. The team's assertiveness served them well and they finished with a very respectable score and were applauded by both Twin City chapters of the NAACP.

Later that spring, the NAACP national office mourned the loss of Charles Hamilton Houston. For the previous generation, Houston had served as a special counsel for the organization and had been largely responsible for developing the strategy to attack the Plessy v. Ferguson's "separate but equal" doctrine.

Houston was born in 1895 in Washington D.C. and was the son of a prominent Howard University professor. He received his B.A. degree and Phi Beta Kappa Key at the age of 19 and went on to earn an L.L.B. degree in 1922 and a D.J.S. degree in 1923. From 1933 to 1935, he served as a member of the District of Columbia's Board of Education. In 1944, he was appointed by President Truman to serve on the President's Committee on Fair Employment Practices. He was probably the greatest unsung hero of the entire modern civil rights era and not only spearheaded the attack, but laid the foundations for the favorable U.S. Supreme Court decisions against restrictive real-estate covenants and against discrimination in schools and colleges.

That summer, Haywood Patterson the last of the nine Scottsboro Boys, was recaptured in Detroit by the FBI, but Governor G. Mennen Williams refused to extradite him to Alabama. He was finally granted a pardon on June 9, 1950.

Later that month, a *Recorder* editorial pointed out that the Catholic Bulletin's caption, "St. Peter Claver Plans New School for Colored Children" was the first time in 60 years in St. Paul that a proposal had been made to segregate African-American children. Newman's challenge caused the Archdiocese to quickly order that a retraction be printed in the next edition.

Later that summer, James Griffin became the first African-American to win a Democratic-Farmer-Labor (DFL) endorsement when he was endorsed as their 38th District Representative by 79 votes in St. Paul. His platform included a call for the enactment of a strong FEPC law.

On the first weekend in July, Mr. and Mrs. Mitchell Rhone, Al Horton and Dorothy Munson were told by the owners of the Avalon excursion steamer that they would not be allowed to come aboard for its weekend midnight cruise as "Negro night" was on the following Wednesday. After some discussion the owners finally accepted their tickets, but told them they would not be allowed to use the dance floor.

Under those conditions, the two couples refused to come aboard and took the matter to the St. Paul NAACP to plan a legal action. The following week, NAACP president J. Nathaniel Smith, filed charges against owner Ernest Meyer and Captain Michael Hall.[2] Both were served with a warrant and pleaded innocent to violating the law. They appeared before Judge Allan S. Pearson on July 7th, and were released on $1,000 bail for Meyer and $200 for Hall. When the case finally came to court, a "laughing and joking" all-white jury returned a verdict of not guilty for owner Meyer and Captain Hall after only 15 minutes of "deliberation." Plaintiffs Rhone and Horton filed civil rights charges against both defendants and subsequently were awarded damages.

In September, irate callers flooded the switchboard of KSTP-TV when host, Marjorie McCrady, of the program, "For You Ladies" instructed one of her fashion models to, "walk like a nigger with a basket of cotton on your head." A station official told the NAACP that the term would never be used again.[3]

The following month, as a result of protests on the part of Clifford E. Rucker, the burial of African-American veterans in segregated plots at Fort Snelling was discontinued. Rucker wrote President Truman on October 9th and received a personal reply a week later from Major General H. Feldman of the Quartermaster General's office who told him that the six remaining plots in the segregated section could be filled with African-American veterans if their survivors so desired, but after that all future burials at Fort Snelling would be on a non-segregated basis.[4]

In November, S. Vincent Owens declared at the Urban League's Annual Dinner that, "It is becoming easier to match African-Americans in St. Paul, to jobs for which they are best qualified." Owens had been instrumental in getting hired an African-American research chemist, Martin Brookins at Rayette, Inc., African-American saleswomen in four downtown department stores, an insurance salesman and African-American streetcar motormen and conductors.

In December, Charles Hamilton Houston was awarded the NAACP's Spingarn Medal, posthumously, for his pioneering work in the field of civil rights.

The following January, a decade long struggle to integrate the state's National Guard ended in 1951 with the swearing in of African-American St. Paulites Theodore Freeze and Delbert Crushon into the 47th Viking Division.[5] Later that summer, before the division left for its annual bivouac, Ashby Gaskins headed a delegation which met with Governor Youngdahl. They expressed to him their concerns that the integrity of the desegregated 47th might be compromised at Camp Rucker, Alabama. Youngdahl, contacted Senator Humphrey, who in turn spoke with Assistant Secretary of the Army, Earle D. Johnson. Humphrey reported back to Gaskins that Johnson had assured him throughout the bivouac, the 47th would remain integrated.

Early in 1951, S. Vincent Owens appeared before the Minnesota Legislature's House Labor Committee to testify for the passage of a state FEPC law. Mr. Owens charged that of the 800 manufacturing firms in St. Paul, only 126 employed African-Americans and only 16 of them used these African-American employees, "in accordance with their skills and abilities." He also declared that in a recent Urban League survey of 257 firms, the League found that 68 percent of them did not employ any African-Americans that 53 percent said they would never employ them and 40 percent said they might employ them sometime in the future.[6]

In May, over 600 white residents of St. Paul's East Side gathered to protest the zoning changes that would make possible the construction of low-rent housing on a site near Wheelock Parkway and Jackson Street. Public Works Commissioner Milton Rosen joined in supporting the group's opposition. After extensive hearing, however the public housing was approved by the City Council.

CHAPTER EIGHT 1950 – 1959

In June, John Marshall High School counselor Pearl Turnquist wrote the Bell Telephone Company to support the employment of African-American student Harriet O'Neal. In her letter, she noted that her former student was "fully capable of handling the position of long-distance telephone operator without having to serve an apprenticeship as an elevator operator as she had been told." As a result, the company agreed to hire Miss O'Neal, as a telephone operator and intended to review their future hiring practices.

In the middle of the month, Frank Boyd, the Secretary-Treasurer of BSCP local for 25 years, was awarded a sum of $2,000 on the eve of the brotherhood's silver jubilee celebration. At the banquet, national President A. Philip Randolph hailed him as, "a true black revolutionist, who as a labor organizer had been an inspiration to his fellow men!"

In August, the passport of civil and human rights leader, Paul Robeson was revoked by the U.S. State Department and Secretary of State Acheson told his lawyer, Nathan Witt, "the Department considers that Robeson's travel abroad, at this time would be contrary to the best interests of the United States."[7]

Also that fall, Governor Luther Youngdahl, after a receiving a report from Clifford Rucker, ordered Prison Director Carl Jackson to desegregate C Block at Stillwater Prison and to end all segregation immediately. Youngdahl also ordered that vocational opportunities be made available to all inmates on a non-discriminatory basis.[8]

Also, the Ten Strike League at St. Paul Claver Bowling Alley, which was managed by Ralph Jones, became one of America's first interracial leagues sanctioned by the American Bowling Congress that fall.

In mid-October, Senator Louis Hill, the son of Minnesota's "Empire Builder," who represented the city's 40th Senatorial District, which contained most of St. Paul's African-American population, voted against the passage of the state FEPC. His actions surprised and angered the city's African-American population and Hill's only explanation was that he thought the problems of minorities, "should be kept theoretical" and though he recognized the fact of discrimination against minorities, all he could say to them at that point was that, "I am sorry." Despite his poor performance in relating to this constituency, the legislature did pass the legislation outlawing discrimination in municipal civil service examinations (Section 44.07-08) and Hill was defeated at the next election.

In December, the Twin Cities African-American community was shocked to hear that University of Minnesota summarily dismissed philosophy professor, Forest Wiggins, an African-American, from his position in the Philosophy Department. Editor Newman, who was an avid anti-communist, took the controversial position of saying in an editorial, "that Wiggins' membership in the Socialist Party gave his enemies ammunition which he should not have allowed to happen." Newman suggested that, "every black, in a responsible position, owes it to himself and his coming generation to conduct himself in an impeccable manner. This will prevent any anti-black segment in the society, from using anything that you say or do against you." This position was rejected by a large segment of his readership. Despite the fact that some university officials attempted to cover his dismissal by calling Wiggins, "incompetent as a teacher and a scholar," his department chairman, George P. Conger, as well as his teaching colleagues commended him as a teacher and 226 of his students signed a statement praising his abilities. Despite their support and that of a considerable part of the community of both cities, Wiggins appeared to have been an early victim of McCarthyism, which was soon destined to sweep the country.[9]

As the year ended, the St. Paul Council of Human Relations re-elected Warren Burger to their Board of Directors.

In January 1952, St. Paul became the first city to host an American Bowling Congress Tournament after the organization dropped its racist policies.[10]

In February, Cecil Newman became the first African-American Minnesotan ever to be listed in the nation's Who's Who in America.

That spring, Firefighter Leroy Coleman was appointed the first African-American Captain of an integrated fire station in St. Paul, and was assigned to Engine Company #15 located at Fairfield and Livingston Streets. Also, Junius Powell became St. Paul's first African-American bus driver to be assigned one of St. Paul's 51 new buses.

In May, largely due to protests of retired heavyweight champion, Joe Louis, whose attempts to play in the San Diego Open created national headlines, the PGA decided to allow African-American golfers, Sol Hughes and Ted Rhodes to play in the St. Paul Open in June, and Rhodes placed 17th among the money winners and received $230.[11] The following month, Rhodes placed 6th in the Chicago's Tam O'Shanter Tournament which was the only major tournament in the country that had previously welcomed African-Americans.

Also in July, Miss Louise Mills, a St. Paul Central High School teacher, who was also a founding member of the St. Paul Council of Human Relations, received the Pledge of American Unity Award, for her work in promoting inter-group education in the city's schools. According to Arnold Rose, a sociology professor at the University of Minnesota, Miss Mills had, "one of the best reference libraries on race and human relations materials in the country."

In August, the Governor's Interracial Commission sponsored an NAACP Human Relations booth at the Minnesota State Fair for the first time. A survey was taken at the booth that asked fair-goers four questions. The first was: "Indians were the original Minnesotans. Should they now have all the rights and privileges and duties of other Minnesota citizens?" The results were 3,464 Yes and 135 No. The second question asked was: "Do you believe in equal employment opportunities for all, regardless of race, religion or national origins?" If so, should there be a state law enforcing this objective?" The results were

3,419 Yes and 353 No. The third question asked was: "Should the teaching of better human relations be included in the curriculum of all public and private schools?" The results were 3,504 Yes and 117 No. The final question asked was: "Do you believe that every person should be treated without discrimination in housing, hospitals, and other public facilities?" The results were 3,455 Yes and 133 No.

In September, Editor Newman said he was going to break a non-endorsement policy of his paper for primary candidates to endorse Jimmy Griffin who was running for the 38th District House seat. He said he was doing it because of how strongly he felt about the worth of Griffin and wanted him to make it through the primary. Although Newman did not endorse Peter Povovich for the 40th Senatorial District seat he did remind voters that the incumbent, Louis Hill, still opposed the passage of the state FEPC and it helped bring about Hill's subsequent defeat. At the fall convention, Mrs. Allie Mae Hampton became the first African-American woman in Minnesota history to be named a national member of the Democratic Farmer-Labor Party.

That fall, the St. Paul community mourned the death of 43-year old S. Vincent Owens, who had been a dedicated social worker and employment advocate with the Urban League for 12 years and who had created more job openings than any of his predecessors, in business, in industry, in clerical and in sales.

He was survived by his wife, Wanda, his son, Sterling, and their three daughters, Wanda Marie, Ermon and Van Hazel. At his funeral, Governor Elmer Anderson noted that, "the state had suffered a great loss and Vincent's contributions toward creating an atmosphere of understanding and better human relations between the people of our state will be long remembered."

Following his burial, a Vincent Owens Memorial Fund was established in cooperation with the University of Minnesota to provide scholarships to graduate social work students interested in doing research in the areas of interracial, intercultural relations.[12]

In November, when the newly elected Eisenhower administration celebrated their victory with 24 percent of the black vote, the Tuskegee Institute also reported good news to African-Americans when it announced that 1952 had been the first year since 1881 that no lynching had been reported in the country. There was also an increase in community activism among St. Paul's African-American religious stalwarts who followed the protest tradition kept alive by Stephen Theobald of St. Peter Claver, Joseph Harris of Memorial Baptist, W. D. Carter, Amos Brown of Pilgrim Baptist, C. F. Stewart of St. James A.M.E. as well as T. R. Nelson and Joseph Pilot of Camphor A.M.E.

As 1953 began, another activist rose to defend the rights of the community. The Reverend Floyd Massey Jr. of Pilgrim Baptist Church rallied a crowd of 125 parents at a St. Paul Board of Education meeting to demand the building of a new elementary school in St. Paul to replace the antiquated Maxfield Elementary School.

Another person who spoke at the meeting was an activist priest who had a distinguished career of union and racial activism dating back to the 1930s. He was Father Francis Gilligan who had been born in Fall River, Massachusetts, in 1898, and had arrived in St. Paul in 1928 after being asked by Archbishop Dowling to join his staff at the St. Paul Seminary. Gilligan had received his Ph.D. in 1924 from the Catholic University of America in Washington D.C. with a dissertation on, "The Morality of the Color Line" which offered a moral code for the equal treatment of African-American people. During the 1930s, he was active in the fight for union rights as well as those for African-American people. As his reputation grew, priests from around the country would telephone him when they knew important African-American people were coming to St. Paul. Some had Gilligan make a reservation for their African-American friends in order to save them from embarrassment by bigoted hotel clerks. Often Gilligan would make the reservations and on the day of their arrival would wait for them in the lobby of their hotel. When the distinguished visitor would make their appearance and ask the desk clerk for their room key, the response was invariably that either the reservation had not been made or that it had been mislaid and that unfortunately no rooms were available. At that point Father Gilligan would step forward and ask the clerk to please check again as he had made the reservation. Without fail the reservation was quickly found and the room would be made available.

In 1943, Gilligan had been appointed by Governor Edward J. Thye to be chairman of the first Governor's Interracial Commission and served faithfully for over a decade. During that time, he had been responsible for all investigations as well as confrontations and negotiations until he had been finally given the assistance of Cliff Rucker in the mid-1940s. In 1949, Gilligan had lobbied for the passage of the first Fair Employment Practices bill despite the criticism from some lobbyists that he was being, "too high-handed and thought he was God," and other criticisms by the African-American community that he was ignoring certain, "strengthening provisions." He continued to serve under Archbishop Dowling, as well as Murray, Bryne, and Roach.

In February, St. Paul native George Holland, who had left his milk driving job in St. Paul to join V.A. Director Carol Gray as his administrative assistant in Washington D.C., was cited by the District of Columbia's American Legion posts, for his, "outstanding contributions in the protection of the rights and welfare of the District's veterans, and their dependents."

Early that spring, St. Paul's largest employer, Minnesota Mining and Manufacturing (3M), gave an unexpected boost to the cause of civil rights when it came out in favor of the passage of a state FEPC bill.

It was also about this time that a check of the Register of Deeds office by the NAACP had disclosed that St. Paul had 25 real estate covenants that restricted the sale of property to whites only. Civil rights leaders were successful in convincing Representative Odean Enestvedt of Renville and Senator Duff to introduce legislation to amend a 1949 law lobbied by Father Gilligan, which covered only religious discrimination in housing and to extend it to also cover race. The bill passed both the House and the Senate and was promptly signed by Governor C. Elmer Anderson.[13]

That spring, largely through the advocacy of the Reverend Massey, Maceo Moody, Jimmy Griffin, William Sayles, Bea Coleman, Nathaniel Gallaway and Lawrence Stewart, the St. Paul School Board voted to construct a new Maxfield School and not to settle for remodeling the old building. Their actions followed a petition of 1,642 interested citizens and parents who had hired an architect to survey the old 1903 structure. Out of their efforts came the first neighborhood district council. It was designed to improve community values and to create better understanding and responsibility within the neighborhood.

In June, when St. Paul's newly appointed Urban League Executive Secretary, Thomas Talley, and his wife were refused service at the Lexington Restaurant, Talley proceeded to bring charges against the establishment.[14] The Grand Jury, which eventually convened, however, returned a "No Bill" after accepting the word of manager, Donald Ryan, who tardily produced a list of reservations, from the day in question, which he claimed to have "forgotten" to submit to the county attorney when he was first questioned.

Later that summer, President Eisenhower issued a statement in which he promised to "use the powers of the federal government to combat and erase racial discrimination and segregation, so that no man of any color or creed will be able to say, 'this is not a free land.'" He followed up his declaration by establishing a Government Contract Compliance Committee to supervise anti-discrimination regulations in government contracts. However, he appointed Vice President Nixon to serve as its chairman and Nixon did not act upon the National NAACP's two major complaints against Capital Transit Company and the Chesapeake and

Potomac Telephone Company. On August 6th, President Eisenhower ordered all Naval Base commanders to desegregate schools on their bases as well as Veterans Administration hospitals though Rep. Adam Clayton Powell registered a protest that Secretary of the Navy Anderson had failed to carry out the orders of the President, "to end segregation at all military installations."[15]

Meanwhile, the St. Paul Urban League continued to wrestle with the problem of relocating 235 African-American families who had been affected by redevelopment in the north-central area. Ernest Cooper, the newly appointed Executive Secretary, after former Executive Secretary Thomas Talley's automobile accident, pointed out that though 8,500 new housing units had been built in St. Paul during the past five years, only 128 had been made available to non-whites.[16]

On the last day of the year, Hulan Jack became the first African-American to hold a major elected position in a major American city when he became President of the Manhattan Borough. Jack ran against St. Paul's first Executive Urban League Secretary, Elmer Carter.

In 1954, the NAACP launched its Fight for Freedom campaign with a goal of totally eliminating discrimination by the year 1963, the Centennial Year of the Emancipation Proclamation. Governor Anderson participated by ordering the removal of all literature from the Minnesota Tourist Bureau that could be construed as having discriminatory language. He also congratulated Father Gilligan for being cited by the Reverend John LaFarge, in his book, *The Manner is Ordinary*, for being, "One of the state's greatest contributors to the cause of civil rights and interracial justice." There was both good and bad news for the African-American workers on the 11 railroads serving St. Paul. The good news was that the Brotherhood of Railroad Trainmen and Carmen had voted to admit them to their ranks. The bad news was that the Pullman Company declared that henceforth the position of Pullman Porter would be open to members of all races, colors and creeds, which ended an African-American monopoly and demonstrated to all the downside of integration.

In February, the St. Paul Urban League proudly announced that over 50 percent of the 2,433 African-American occupied homes in St. Paul were owned by African-Americans. Also that month, McCarthyite victim, Forest Wiggins, decided not to contest his wife's suit for divorce and after a short stint at Allen University in Columbia, South Carolina, became an expatriate in Mexico.[17]

In the nation's capitol, President Eisenhower appointed J. Ernest Wilkins to the post of Assistant Secretary of Labor making him the first African-American appointee to hold a sub-cabinet post. The next month, Wilkins became the first African-American to attend a President's Cabinet meeting when he substituted for his boss, James Mitchell. In the Congress, the only civil rights bill with enforcement powers was sponsored by Senators Humphrey of Minnesota and Ives of New York and was reported favorably out of the Senate Labor Committee, but was never taken up by the Senate. In May, the U.S. Supreme court handed down its historic landmark decision in Brown v. the Board of Education of Topeka, Kansas. Chief Justice Warren who declared that "separate, but equal" educational facilities were "inherently unequal" and that school segregation was therefore unconstitutional in the plaintiff states of Texas, Oklahoma, Kentucky, Kansas and the District of Columbia wrote the unanimous decision. The desegregation of the schools in the District of Columbia, was particularly gratifying to activist Mary Church Terrell who, in 1895, had been the first African-American woman to be appointed to a school board in America. Fifty-eight years later, she had headed a civil rights group that had finally convinced that later board to both accept and implement desegregation.

Chief Counsel, Thurgood Marshall, along with George E. C. Hayes, and James M. Nabrit, Jr., had argued the Brown Case. Professor Kenneth Clark provided valuable psychological and sociological research. The first five southern states to announce the beginning of desegregation in their schools were West Virginia, Missouri, Arkansas, Maryland and Delaware.

Shortly after the school decision had been made, the National Board of the YMCA adopted a resolution that, "segregation would be eliminated from all YMCA facilities nationwide."[18]

That summer, the Twin City African-American community received another "backlash" from the joys of integration when the annual Bronze Golf Tournament became a Minnesota Negro Open Golf Tournament after being criticized by the state NAACP. Opening the tourna-

Thurgood Marshall

ment to white golfers caused some of them to look upon it as "easy pickings" and for the next few years it caused the number of African-American prizewinners to drastically decrease.

That fall, President Eisenhower ordered the desegregation of all schools on military posts to be completed by the following September. He also announced that as of August 13, "No all-Negro units existed in the armed services of the United States," though many bases continued to evade integration.[19] In October, just before the fall elections, Benjamin O. Davis, Jr. was promoted to Brigadier General by President Eisenhower just as his father had been 14 years before by President Roosevelt. Davis's appointment as the first African-American U.S. Air Force General served to help Republicans in their mid-term elections.

Perhaps one of the most significant examples of agitation and provocation that ever took place in the congress happened in January 1955, when Representative Adam Clayton Powell, of New York, first offered his anti-segregation amendment to a military reserve bill which had declared that all state, territorial or district national guards or air national guards, "must not exclude nor segregate against any person on the basis of race, creed, color or national origin, in the carrying out of its provisions." President Eisenhower, immediately expressed "grave disapproval" to such a proposal of "tacking on social legislation" to something that was so vital to the "security of the nation."[20] Eisenhower rallied his Republican majority to defeat the amendment on July 4th. Also that month the first Citizens Councils were being formed in the South, beginning in Indianola, Mississippi. By October, a statewide association had been formed with over 80,000 members. Their major purpose was to resist school integration and their leadership came largely from the middle-class who didn't hesitate to use their local K.K.K. Klaverns as their enforcing arm. These councils were also responsible for permitting only 8,000 African-Americans to cast ballots in Mississippi out of a total African-American voting-age population of nearly one million. In September, President Eisenhower desegregated the Washington D.C. Fire Department.

In a study completed in early 1955 by the newly appointed St. Paul Urban League Industrial Secretary Richard Fox, found that only 150 out of 800 city firms utilized African-American workers on the basis of their skills and abilities with no restrictions on their placement or up-grading. He also found that the annual income differential between African-American and white workers was $650. 60 of the 150 firms in compliance were being evaluated by the Presidents' Committee on Government Contract Compliance with the help of the St. Paul FEPC.[21]

During the opera season that year, soprano Leontyne Price became the first African-American to gain an opportunity to sing a title role of an opera when she appeared on NBC-TV in the title role in "Tosca." Soon after her appearance, Robert McFerrin, a young African-American baritone, was offered the role of Amerasro in "Aida" at the Metropolitan Opera House, to become the first African-American male to appear in a major operatic role in America. Once the ice was broken, Marian Anderson, who unfortunately was far past her prime, was belatedly offered the role of Ulrica in Verdi's "Un Ballo in Maschera" by the Metropolitan Opera Company later that season.

During the winter quarter, James Phillips and Earl McGee were both offered secondary positions in the St. Paul School System to become the third and fourth African-American teachers to be hired in the 20th century to teach at that level. Phillips had earned a B.S. degree from Indiana University and held an M.A. degree from Columbia Teachers College and was working on his PhD when he was hired to teach ninth grade core curriculum at Cleveland Junior High School. McGee had received his B.S. degree from Macalester College in Commercial Education with a minor in Latin and English literature, but was offered only special education classes to teach at Central High School.

That spring Minnesota became the ninth state to adopt a Fair Employment Practices Law, with full enforcement provisions. Governor Orville L. Freeman signed the bill and also rewarded Richard Fox for his fine work as the St. Paul Urban League Industrial Secretary by appointing him the Assistant Director of the city's Human Rights Commission. Fox was an Indiana University graduate who had been largely responsible for the St. Paul Urban League being chosen one of only four organizations to receive a NAACP National Thalheimer Award for having an outstanding vocational guidance programs for African-American youth.

In St. Paul, Mayor Joseph Dillon selected both Mrs. Alpha Adkins and Mrs. Allie Mae Hampton to serve on the local FEPC Commission. Mrs. Hampton was the president of the Ramsey County DFL Forum and was a shop steward at Simon and Mogilner Company.

That spring, State Attorney General Miles Lord also appointed James Bradford to his staff as the state's first African-American Assistant Attorney General.

That summer, Roy Wilkins, who had recently taken over the leadership of the NAACP from Walter White, reported that over a quarter of a million African-American and white children were now attending school together for the first time in Washington D.C., Maryland, Arkansas, West Virginia, Missouri, Delaware, Kansas, Arizona and New Mexico. He also noted, however, that it was increasingly apparent to many that the U.S. Supreme Court's decision had lacked the kind of guidelines and decisiveness necessary for successful integration. The Court had simply issued orders remanding those cases, which had been under consideration to the lower courts and had failed to give any specific suggestions, such as

Roy Wilkins

progressive desegregation, which might have eased the transition. Instead the Court continued to merely urge the district courts to proceed, "with all deliberate speed," which to many meant "as slow as possible."

That fall, the three-year hiatus America had enjoyed from the hellish practice of public lynchings ended with two murders in the state of Mississippi. The one that shocked the nation the most was the murder of 14 year-old Emmett Louis Till, who was visiting his relatives in Money, Mississippi. Emmett had been lynched because he had allegedly acted "improperly" toward a white woman. He whistled at her. He was subsequently beaten, killed and almost buried by Roy Bryant and J.W. Milan, both of whom were later acquitted by a jury in Money. Fortunately, Emmett's uncle had interrupted the attempts to bury his nephew's mangled body and misshapen head and was later shipped to his mother in Chicago, where thousands viewed it at a public funeral.

Also in Humphrey County, Mississippi, the Reverend George W. Lee was lynched after he and Gus Courts had led a voter registration drive and convinced about 400 of the 15,012 African-Americans of voting age to try and register. After Lee's murder, Courts' name was the only African-American who remained on the voter registration lists as the others had all fallen victim to either physical or economic intimidation.

On November 25th, Courts was a victim of an assassination attempt and was forced to flee. As a result of the terror tactics practiced by white Mississippians, the massive under-registration of African-American voters had been reduced statewide, from 22,000 to 8,000 in less than a year.[22]

Also in November, NAACP Washington Bureau Chief Clarence Mitchell was one of the leading attorneys who brought a suit to the U.S. Supreme Court that resulted in ending segregation in much of the nation's public parks, playgrounds, swimming beaches and golf courses.[23]

Sweeping as it was, the decision had little effect on the real cornerstone of American racism that was contained in the special clause of the handbook of the National Association of Real Estate Boards (NAREB) which states, "A realtor should never be instrumental in introducing a character of property or occupancy of any nature (euphuism for persons of color) which will be detrimental to the property values of a neighborhood…" Walter White had mentioned it in his book, *How Far the Promised Land* and emphasized that the leadership of the NAREB had been largely responsible for blocking all funds in preventing the Federal Housing Administration (FHA) from underwriting any residential building where there were, "incompatible racial and social groups present."[24]

Later that month, Congress did manage to pass the Metcalf-Baker bill with a Powell amendment, which forbade discrimination in housing that was assisted by either FHA or VA funds.

In December, the American Federation of Labor (AFL) and the Congress of Industrial Organizations (CIO) elected both A. Philip Randolph and Willard Townsend to represent the two newly merged unions. Randolph had organized the Pullman porters and had been a member of the industrial union for many years and had been responsible for organizing the nation's Red Caps into a cohesive union.

CHAPTER EIGHT 1950 – 1959

On December 5th, Mrs. Rosa Parks, a seamstress from Montgomery, Alabama, who refused to move to the back of a bus, was arrested for defying a segregation law. Ed Nixon, NAACP President, later bailed her out. Her actions resulted in a year-long boycott by 40,000 African-American residents and served as a catalyst for civil rights era of passive resistance and direct action throughout the South.

On December 23rd, the U.S. Supreme Court failed to come to the aid of Montgomery citizens, but did order the Federal Commerce Commission to end Jim-Crow travel on interstate rail transportation and expanded their previous ruling. It was a Christmas present for millions of African-American travelers who for decades had been forced to travel inhumanely in dirty-smoke-filled coaches if they visited southern states. It was a shocking experience for African-Americans from the North, to discover that the Mason-Dixon Line divided the "Land of Lincoln" into two separate worlds for people of color.

In January 1956, Representative Adam Clayton Powell was physically attacked on the floor of the House Representatives. Cleveland Bailey of West Virginia continually objected to Powell's advocacy of desegregated schools, which was strange in light of the fact that his state was the first to desegregate and with the least amount of opposition. During this month, Rosa Parks was fined one dollar for, "violating an Alabama state law requiring segregation on buses."[25]

In March, Newman reminded his African-American readers to observe, "National Negro Press Week" which he said, "Since 1837, had been the freest press in America." He also declared that African-American people in the United States now had a purchasing power of 16 billion dollars and should use it to gain their freedom.

Near the end of the month, the St. Paul NAACP boasted that it had passed the 1,000 membership mark for the first time in its history as well as signing up their first Life Member, Carl Wescheke, who had led their drive in the State Legislature for "Open Occupancy." Robert Patterson led all recruiters by signing up 162 of the branches' 1,347 members.

In May, St. Paul, which had just been named an All-American City by the National Municipal League, was caught up in a notorious "black bed" controversy. The issue was started by white fire captain, Matt Remackel, who had insisted that a second bed be provided for rotating captains at all fire stations which would be reserved for white captains only. Station #15, where African-American captain Leroy Coleman served, vigorously protested the request for a "white bed." NAACP President Frank Smith, contended that such an arrangement would restrict the training capabilities of African-American fire captains and limit their promotions. After much debate and discussion, Assistant Fire Chief John Barry, told Captain Remackel that his "white bed" had been removed from his quarters and would not be replaced.[26]

That fall, at the urging of Frank Smith, the City Council passed a resolution favoring an ordinance that would ban all racial or religious discrimination in both public and private housing. The passage of Smith's resolution had been largely due to the survey that private citizens had done, which had shown that the proposed I-94 freeway would displace 1,523 persons and included 373 families, 757 adults and 379 children, many of whom were minorities.

The St. Paul Branch of the NAACP threatened to seek an injunction, at one point, against the state highway department, "because of the great differences between the court and state property appraisals and the difficulty of relocating minorities in the outer rim." They felt the proposed freeway would also displace at least 20 African-American businesses and clubs, which would have great difficulty in relocating.

Late in September, ex-heavyweight champion Joe Louis, who in his prime had donated millions to the government during the war years in boxing exhibitions for war bond rallies, was told by the Internal Revenue Department that he still owed them $1,243,097 in back taxes and was told that the IRS intended to take over a $654,000 trust fund that he had set up for the education of his children. Joe, who lamented the fact that his debt, "seems to go up by the minute," said he had been forced to turn to professional wrestling to keep up the payments and in the process had sustained a severe head injury and strained heart muscles which caused his doctors to warn him to stop or he would risk permanent impairment.[27]

In November, the St. Paul FEPC heard complaints about discrimination at Murphy Motor Freight. Their Personnel Director, Carl Bostrom, not only refused to release any personnel files, but also destroyed the complaints. Later that month, the commission found Woolworth's store guilty of violating the ordinance also. A suit was brought by Arthur Cunningham who had applied for a job as a merchandise demonstrator. During the investigation the word "colored" was found on his job application in violation of the ordinance.[28]

The Eisenhower administration reaped the benefits of the 1954 decision despite the fact that Eisenhower had later said, "the appointment of Earl Warren, as Chief Justice, was the worst mistake I ever made as President." The Republican Party managed to garner 40 percent of the black vote as Adlai Stevenson went down to defeat a second time.

On November 13th, in the NAACP's case of Gayle v. Browder the U.S. Supreme Court, explicitly overruled Plessy v. Ferguson and rejected Alabama's appeal while affirming the lower court's ruling in support of King's boycott. Thus ended the 382-day ordeal with King becoming the first passenger to ride an integrated bus in Montgomery, Alabama, bringing an end to Jim-Crow transit throughout the South.

In March 1957, City Councilman Milton Rosen, who was the president of the Minnesota Chapter of B'nai B'rith, told newspaper reporters in Birmingham, Alabama that, "Before I came here I had the impression that Negroes were down-trodden and in a suppressed condition in the South. However, on this visit I have seen Negro schools, golf courses and swimming pools. Rabble rousers have told us that Negroes are terribly mistreated. It's a whole lot of misinformation!" When he returned to St. Paul, Rosen's statements were denounced by the St. Paul Jewish Council, as well as the Reverends Floyd Massey and Denzil Carty, and both Frank Smith and Leonard Carter of the NAACP.[29]

In April, after extensive lobbying by Reverend Denzil Carty, Ernest Cooper, Louis Ervin, Stephen Maxwell and Maymie Green, the State Senate judiciary committee approved an open occupancy bill (Senate File #1351) without a dissenting vote. They were assisted in their efforts by L. Howard Bennett, Clifford Rucker, Shelton Granger, Wilfred Leland and Mrs. Nate Crabtree. The bill was authored by Senator Don Fraser.

In June, Dovdal H. Davis, the general Manager of the Kansas City Call, died. He had joined the Call's staff in 1939 and had originated the annual Russwurm Award of the National Newspaper Publishers Association (NNPA), which had been given to persons, organizations or institutions who had made, "significant contributions to a more democratic life in the United States."

In July, Althea Gibson became the first woman of color to win the Wimbledon Tennis Championship. Newspapers had criticized the crowd for the poor manners they had shown her during the early rounds of the tournament. Queen Elizabeth for the first time in her reign attended the championship match and the crowds were better behaved. She presented the trophy. Althea was later chosen to be a member of the U.S. Wightman Cup Team who went on to win the Cup.

In August, Congress passed its first civil rights legislation since 1875, with a bill (H.R. 6127) that established a Federal Civil Rights Commission and gave a division of the Justice Department the authority to seek injunctions against voting rights infractions. The bill passed the House by a 266 to 126 margin with Minnesota Representatives Blatnik, Knutson, Marshall and Weir voting for it but it was defeated in the Senate 52–38 with Senator Eugene McCarthy voting for it. Unfortunately, Title III was stripped of its equal protection rights under the Fourteenth Amendment in a Conference Committee while Title IV was weakened by the addition of a jury trial amendment for voting violations, when everyone knew that throughout most of the South African-Americans were ignored for jury duty. The Senators who voted to weaken Title III and IV before its passage included Democrats Paul Church of Idaho, John Kennedy of Massachusetts and Dennis Chavez of New Mexico. During the debate over the bill, Senator Paul Douglas of Illinois, reported that 96.1 percent of Mississippi's African-Americans were forbidden to vote or to serve on juries, 89.7 percent in Alabama, 85.3 percent in Arkansas, 79.9 percent in Virginia, 79.1 percent in Texas, 74.7 percent in South Carolina, 71.5 percent in Georgia, 66.5 percent in Louisiana and 59.8 percent in Florida. Douglas told the Senate that in Mississippi, less than 7,000 African-Americans could vote out of a total population of over a million.[30]

That summer, Pope Pius XII appointed Father Francis J. Gilligan, a Monsignor. Most civil rights advocates in the Saintly City rejoiced as he had been one of the most dedicated of the early civil rights advocates in the city and had been an activist during the past three decades. He had also been an important instrument in educating St. Paul's white Catholic population about racial matters. Gilligan was not only critical of tokenism, but often chided St. Paul businessmen for not reaching out to their African-American employees and to the post office for resisting efforts to have African-Americans as postal window clerks. During the years he had also been helpful in getting the Minnesota Legislature to pass Sec. 953.1 and 953.2, which declared, "practices of discrimination and segregation in housing were against the public policy of Minnesota and declared fair housing a civil right."

In the fall of 1957, St. Paul members at the 41st Annual Meeting of the American Federation of Teachers had their moment of civic greatness when they refused to bow to the pressure from southern locals and insisted, along with other colleagues, that they must integrate as of January 1st or be dropped. 1,855 members of the Atlanta local chose to withdraw from the parent organization.

In September, Reverend Denzil Carty, Leonard Carter and Jerry Robbins were able to exert enough pressure on the local DFL leadership to have them cancel the invitation to Senator Paul Church, to speak at the Franklin D. Roosevelt Memorial Dinner. Church had voted against Section III of the Civil Rights bill, which would have given African-Americans in the South the right to serve on juries regardless of whether they were registered voters.

Rev. Denzil Carty

In December, Governor Freeman appointed D. Howard Bennett as the state's first African-American municipal judge. Bennett had graduated from the University of Chicago with a Doctor of Laws degree. In 1950, he was also made a member of the American Council on Race Relations shortly after he moved to the Twin Cities where he became a member of the Hall, Smith, Hedlund, Juster and Forsburg Law Firm.

As 1958 began, Timothy Howard, President of the Rondo-St. Anthony Freeway Association was honored at a dinner given by the association, "for the yeoman work he had done for twelve months on behalf of the citizens displaced by the freeway." All agreed that he had given long hours of dedicated effort of protest against the $9,000.00 monetary limitation of Section 221 of the Federal Housing Authority which prevents most displaced residents from re-building equitable or even adequate homes.

The following month the St. Paul NAACP noted that the city now had the semblance of a full-blown ghetto with 93 percent of its 7,000 black residents now living in an area bounded by Aurora and Dayton Avenues on its north and south sides and Lexington Parkway and Western Avenue on its west and east sides.[31]

Also that month, African-American Attorney Stephen Maxwell successfully argued a discrimination case against Duke's Café in Inver Grove Heights. The plaintiffs, Robert Crewe and Sidney Richardson, were each awarded $400.

At the end of the month, 400 angry African-American citizens attended the St. Paul City Council hearing on open occupancy, which resulted in the Council sending a citizens' proposed ordinance to their Corporation Counsel for study.

That fall, Governor Orville Freeman was invited to address the first National Convention of the Catholic Interracial Councils in Chicago. He was introduced by Father John LaFarge, the founder of the National Conference for Interracial Justice and though Freeman was a Lutheran, Lafarge said he had been invited because of his, "consistent support of civil and human rights." On November 19th, Freeman designated it as Equal Opportunity Day at the behest of the St. Paul Urban League.

Another event that fall was when restaurateur Benjamin Berger set up a Minnesota Prisoner's Aid Society with Allen Eubanks as its Executive Secretary to help protect the human rights of Minnesota prisoners and parolees and to help build public support for their welfare. He asked Judge Luther Youngdahl to speak at their first annual dinner.

Murphy Motor Freight Company, after repeated violations of fair employment practices, was finally found guilty that fall of using unfair employment practices by the St. Paul FEPC and was ordered to rehire its most recent defendant, Charles Williams, if he reapplied within four months.

In December, Ramsey County Attorney William Randall appointed Stephen Maxwell his assistant county attorney.

As the state's Centennial year drew to a close, African-American editor Mary Kyle of the *Twin City Observer* wrote:

> Galling chains were quickly shattered
> In this land of lakes and forest,
> And the black man walked unhampered
> Over hills and fields and valleys
>
> Years rolled on and education
> Thrust aside the veil of ignorance
> Fitted him for skilled professions
> Beckoned him toward new horizons.
>
> Years of progress lie behind him,
> Years ahead hold faith and courage.[32]

As the last year of the decade began, NAACP President Leonard Carter welcomed the news that the Urban Renewal Administration had dropped its quota for low-cost 221 housing which previously had restricted occupancy.

The following month, Carter spoke on the Mel Jass' Open House program in favor of open occupancy housing and praised the Twin City Council of Clubs for their canvass of St. Paul neighborhoods asking support for the legislation.

Also in February, Mrs. Ethel (Howard) Maxwell Williams died. She had been one of the first African-American women in the state to gain prominence in the field of social work. During World War II, she had served as an Industrial Relations Specialist at the Twin City Federal Cartridge Corporation and had been instrumental in helping integrate African-American workers into new job classifications.

In April, the St. Paul NAACP attacked the provision approved by the Minnesota State Fair Employment Practices Commission that would allow state fair employers' to require photographs of applicants prior to their interviews. Carter told reporters that the NAACP had hopes of eliminating the offensive provision in the next legislative session.

In May, at a St. Paul City Council meeting on housing discrimination, Clayton Rein, Kennon v. Rothschild, John Greenman and Jack Plaff all endorsed the need for an ordinance dealing with housing bias. Shirley Rehnwall, the Executive Secretary of the Minnesota Homeowners Association, which had 5,000 members, said she thought those who favored open occupancy "were trying to push things too fast." At the meeting, Ernest Cooper, the Executive Director of the St. Paul Urban League told the council that the Board of Realtor's statement was a delaying tactic and that he had found nothing in the past practices of the MHA or the St. Paul Board of Realtors that suggested they wished to eliminate housing discrimination.[33]

That summer, Minnesota Republican bar association members, who were miffed because they had not been consulted before Governor Freeman made his appointment of Judge L. Howard Bennett, decided to run their very popular past president, Elmer R. Anderson, against him. Anderson easily defeated Bennett and African-American Minnesotans lost their only judge.

Later that summer, Timothy Howard was named "Man of the Year" by the Layman's Branch of the National Baptist Convention for his work with citizens displaced by the freeway construction in St. Paul. He was also accorded a reception at Pilgrim Baptist Church for his work as President of the Rondo-St. Anthony Association and lauded for his work in assisting many of the 435 displaced homeowners to get their proper monetary awards, by interceding with the St. Paul Housing Authority to help resolve their claims. He was also cited for his efforts along with Father Luger of St. Peter Claver Church in convincing the highway department to depress the freeway and thus make it less noxious to the community. He was nominated by Benjamin Taylor and was the first St. Paulite ever to win the coveted award from the Baptist churchmen.[34]

In September, Sandy Stephens of the University of Minnesota football squad became the first African-American starting quarterback in Big Ten history.[35] Cecil Newman took the occasion to criticize the University's basketball coach, Ozzie Cowles, who had never played an African-American basketball player during his 12-year tenure. Newman noted that this ban included his ignoring the talents of Cozelle Breelove, and Kenneth "Puzzy" Wallace who were all-city high school players in Minneapolis and L.C. Hester, of Duluth.

Also in September, Leonard Carter was chosen Regional Field Director for the NAACP mainly because of his, "courage, imagination, honesty, energy, humor, and articulation of civil rights issues while carrying out his duties in St. Paul."

Near the end of the month, the St. Paul City Council, voted 4–3 to uphold the right of fire captain LeRoy Coleman to build a home on Wheelock Parkway. The council had been asked to confiscate Coleman's property and use it for a public park despite the fact that in 1956, when the same proposal was made concerning the same parcel of land, it had been rejected by the council.

On the Feast Day of Christ the King in October, the St. Paul Catholic Interracial Council held its first workshop at St. Thomas College. Monsignor Louis J. McCarthy gave the major address to the 170 persons present. Two months later, a national organization of 34 councils was formed in Chicago, with Dr. John J. O'Connors as its first President, Charles Wexler as Treasurer and Matthew Ahmann as the first Executive Director.

In December, at the American Legion Fall Conference, at the Hotel St. Paul, committee member, Dan Foley announced that National Commander Martin B. McNally had revoked the right of the 40 and 8 subsidiary organization to use the name or the emblem of the American Legion and told the assembled group that, "we can no longer tolerate the blatant undermining of democratic principles by the 'White Only' clause of the 40 and 8 society." Some credit for its enactment must go to St. Paul's Martin Weddington, who testified against it at the previous national convention.[36]

Also that month, Monsignor Gilligan volunteered to serve as the spiritual advisor for the fledgling Twin City Catholic Interracial Council. Arthur McWatt was elected treasurer and chief fundraiser for the Council. Through this organization, its members hoped to bring the spirit of Christian Brotherhood and Interracial Justice to the Twin City parishes. Gilligan had brought a deep commitment of these concepts to many Catholics while serving under Archbishops Dowling, Murray, Byrne, Brady and Roach.

On the national level, the U.S. Supreme Court's affirmation of the Browder v. Gale bus-boycott Montgomery, desegregation decision evoked a mass awakening of African-American aspirations throughout the South. The victory demonstrated how a disciplined unity of purpose could achieve victory over uncompromising racism. Their efforts were enhanced by the trailblazing efforts of Fifth Circuit Judges, Frank M. Johnson, and his "Four Horsemen of Civil Rights, Richard Rives, Elbert Tuttle, Minor Wisdom and John R. Brown,"[37] who together shared an unshakable belief that the Fourteenth Amendment provided the authority and the Brown judgment the mandate to strike down much of the South's caste system which denied equality to its African-American population.

Another important advancement was the integration of the armed services in the late fifties which precipitated the integration of Minnesota's own National Guard by Governor Luther Youngdahl. This was followed by the integration of burial plots at the Fort Snelling cemetery as well as the desegregation at our state prison at Stillwater. There was also movement in the hiring of new teachers of color, which resulted in the appointment of Arthur McWatt in 1956 to Marshall Junior High School. McWatt became only the fifth African-American secondary teacher to be hired by the St. Paul School Board. It was a time during which many of the city's African-American ministers formed the Ministerial Alliance, which later spearheaded many community protests in defense of civil rights.

These advancements were tempered by the crisis that resulted from the construction of Interstate 94, which had a divisive effect on the social, economic and spiritual life of the community and exacerbated an already critical housing shortage.

CHAPTER EIGHT BIBLIOGRAPHY

1. Berman, Peter M. *The Negro in America*, p. 522.

2. *St. Paul Recorder*, 7 July 1950.

3. *St. Paul Recorder*, 1 September 1950.

4. *St. Paul Recorder*, 6 October 1950.

5. *St. Paul Recorder*, 19 January 1951.

6. *St. Paul Recorder*, 2 February 1951.

7. Duberman, Martin, *Paul Robeson: A Biography*, The New Press, New York, 1989, p. 389.

8. *St. Paul Recorder*, 14 September 1951.

9. *St. Paul Recorder*, 21 December 1951.

10. *St. Paul Recorder*, 18 January 1952.

1. *St. Paul Recorder*, 4 July 1952.

11. Interview with Charles Rogers, 1 June 1995.

12. *St. Paul Recorder*, 24 April 1953.

13. *St. Paul Recorder*, 19 June 1953.

14. *St. Paul Recorder*, 14 August 1953.

15. *St. Paul Recorder*, 18 December 1953.

16. *St. Paul Recorder,* 19 February 1954.

17. *St. Paul Recorder*, 25 June 1954.

18. Watson, Denton L. *Lion in the Lobby: Clarence Mitchell Jr.'s Struggle for the Passage of Civil Rights Laws*, William Morrow and Company Inc., New York, 1991, p. 240.

19. *St. Paul Recorder*, 19 January 1955.

20. *St. Paul Recorder*, 25 February 1955.

21. Bergman, Peter M., *The Negro in America*, p. 543.

22. *St. Paul Recorder*, 11 November 1955.

23. *St. Paul Recorder*, 18 November 1955.

24. *St. Paul Recorder*, 13 January 1956.

25. *St. Paul Recorder*, 18 May 1956.

26. *St. Paul Recorder*, 7 September 1956.

27. *St. Paul Recorder*, 5 October 1956.

28. *St. Paul Recorder*, 1 March 1957.

29. *St. Paul Recorder*, 21 June 1957.

30. *St. Paul Recorder*, 28 February 1958.

31. *Twin City Observer*, 23 December 1958.

32. *Twin City Observer*, 23 May 1959.

33. *St. Paul Recorder*, 28 August 1959.

34. *St. Paul Recorder*, 25 September 1959.

35. *St. Paul Recorder*, 11 December 1959.

36. Bass, Jack, Taming t*he Storm: The Life and Times of Judge Frank M. Johnson, J., and the South's Fight over Civil Rights*, Anchor Books, Doubleday, New York, 1993, p. 133.

37. Bass, Jack, *Taming the Storm: The Life and Times of Judge Frank M. Johnson, J., and the South's Fight over Civil Rights*, Anchor Books, Doubleday, New York, 1993.

Chapter Nine
1960 – 1969

"Our people have sometimes made the mistake of confusing the methods with the objectives, we should never fall out with each other because we believe in different methods or tactics or strategies. We have to keep in mind, at all times that we are not fighting for integration, nor are we fighting for separation. We are fighting for recognition as free human beings in this society."

Malcolm X

On February 1, 1960, four students from North Carolina A & T College began a sit-in movement in Greensboro, at a five and dime store that soon spread to 15 southern cities and to five states. The Student Nonviolent Coordinating Committee was formed in Atlanta and church kneel-ins, beach wade-ins and lunch counter and bus station sit-ins swept the South. By the end of March, San Antonio, Texas had become the first southern city to integrate its lunch counters.[1]

In Minnesota, Governor Freeman recognized the importance of the new phenomena and made plans to host 22 Midwestern governors at a conference on civil rights the following month.

Local NAACP president Addie Few announced that the St. Paul chapter would start picketing Woolworth stores on April 2nd and noted that nationwide picketing had caused a 9 percent sales drop by the end of March.[2]

On May 6th, President Eisenhower signed a new 1960 Civil Rights Law as well as legislation that would authorize federal judges to appoint referees to aid African-Americans in registering to vote for federal elections. The legislation also outlawed mob actions used to restrict voting. Unfortunately, at the same news conference, he appointed John H.

Hannah as the national civil rights commissioner who announced that he was, "opposed to Negroes demonstrating against northern chain stores."[3]

The idea of bringing a NAACP National Convention to St. Paul had really begun in 1958 when Leonard Carter, Carl Weshske, J. Nathaniel Smith, Robert Patterson, Father Denzil Carty, Majorie Tolliver and President Don Lewis began their lobbying efforts at the Cleveland convention with the theme, "Bring Roy Home!" Their rallying cry was so successful that by the second day of the convention they had won over the delegates. In June, Lewis supervised the 18 committees of over 200 members while still managing to organize the barbecuing of 2,000 pounds of ribs over a pit ten feet deep and ten feet long on Harriet Island. The cooks worked in shifts for 72 hours to provide food for the 2,000 delegates. Margaret Belafonte organized a fashion show. The keynote speaker was A. Philip Randolph of the BSCP.

A high point of the convention for Roy Wilkins was when 600 Youth Council delegates demonstrated their support for him by sweeping him off his feet and carrying him around the convention hall on their shoulders. Wilkins had become sensitive to the criticism he had been receiving from Student Nonviolent Coordinating Committee members (SNCC) as well as the younger members of Congress of Racial Equality (CORE). It was so overwhelming that the gesture brought tears to eyes of 80-year old Arthur Spingarn.

As a result of the convention, St. Paul's white citizens gained a new awareness of the city's 8,240 African-American citizens as well as the interracial nature of the NAACP and its success in raising local membership to over 3000.

As the convention came to a close, Clarence Mitchell III, son of Clarence Mitchell II, DC's NAACP Director's son, had been lionized there for both his civil rights accomplishments as a Morgan State student and for being a St. Paul native. Mitchell was struck by the sharp contrast between what his father had characterized as the "subterranean" nature of St. Paul's racism and the blatant segregation, which existed around Morgan State in Baltimore. Mitchell was so inspired, that a week after he returned home, he was arrested for demonstrating against Miller Brothers Restaurant where its outer wall depicted it as a former slave market. The sign was eventually removed.[4]

In July, Editor Newman decided not to cover the Democratic Convention after his friend Humphrey had been forced out of the race by Kennedy plus the fact that only 82 African-American delegates were in attendance.

That fall, in response to pleas by the local NAACP, citizens of St. Paul sent food and clothing to the African-American citizens of Fayette County, Tennessee, who had been subjected to both economic and physical reprisals for having tried to register to vote. Their bank credit had been stopped, mortgages had been foreclosed and gas stations had refused them service for farm work.

In October, the Woolworth, Kresge and Grant stores issued a joint statement in St. Paul, that they were integrating their lunch counters in 12 southern states and in 112 cities and towns.[5]

In November, the Reverend Denzil Carty, who was president of both the Minnesota State Conference of the NAACP and the St. Paul Urban League, received the "President of the Year" Award at the annual President's Ball.

Denzil A. Carty was born at St. Johns, Antigua, the British West Indies in March 1904. He received his early education in Antigua, but moved with his family to New York City around 1922 where he attended high school at Washington Heights and graduated valedictorian in 1925. He then attended New York City College where he was a president of the Frederick Douglass Debating Society before receiving his B.S. degree in Education. He then attended General Theological Seminary in New York City where he received his S.T.B. degree in 1934.

He was assigned as a Curate to All Souls Church that year, which was then located on 114th Street. The church had a predominately white congregation though African-Americans were allowed to worship on a segregated basis. Carty objected to this arrangement and invited African-American members to integrate and the vestry responded by padlocking the door. Carty convinced Bishop Manning to come and resolve the conflict and the Bishop dramatically broke the padlock with a hammer. Carty was then appointed Curate of St. Phillips Church in New York City where he served for a short time before becoming Vicar of St. Luke Chapel before his induction into the U.S. Army in 1944 as a Chaplain. He was assigned to the 512th Port Battalion, which eventually went overseas and was stationed at Southampton on the English coast. The battalion helped bring up supplies for the invasion of Normandy and in its aftermath Carty was the only African-American chaplain to officiate at the burial at Brookfield Cemetery.

He was discharged from the army as a captain in 1946 and after completing his graduate work in Clinical Psychology at Wayne State University in Detroit, was assigned to St. Phillips Episcopal Church in St. Paul. He moved there with his wife, Sylvia, and his daughters, Denise, Jacqueline and Celeste, to live at the rectory located on Mackubin and Aurora Streets. He became active in interracial matters and his soft-spoken voice with the faint English accent began to be increasingly heard by Twin Citians speaking out for social justice over both radio and television stations. When he first joined the NAACP, he was elected chairman of their housing and personnel committees. He was also responsible for setting up a Department of Christian Social Relations for the Episcopal Diocese.

In the last half of the decade, he was instrumental in the lobbying efforts to pass the Fair Employment Practices Law and having a "penalty provision" inserted which impressed Governor Anderson. He was also appointed to the St. Paul Council of Human Relations, along with his duties on both the State Human Rights Commission and the FEPC Commissions' Boards of Review.

In November, the two million leaflets describing Kennedy's intervention in Dr. Martin Luther King, Jr.'s jailing and his call to King's wife, Corretta, and Bobby Kennedy's call to Judge Oscar Mitchell with a request to release him on bail, helped edge out Richard Nixon by 112,881 votes and JFK won 68 percent of the African-American vote, which was a 7 percent increase over Adlai Stevenson's 1956 tally.[6]

Martin Luther King Jr.

In January 1961, Clifford Rucker, who had replaced Monsignor Gilligan as the Executive Director of the Governor's Human Rights Commission, announced that he had established advisory committees of 200 persons or more, in 13 key cities throughout the state to help implement civil rights legislation.

In February, Dan Jacobowski, the director of the St. Paul FEPC reported processing 73 cases of discrimination in 1960, with three-fourths of them dealing with private employers, one-fifth with government agencies and the remainder with either employment agencies or labor unions.[7]

On March 6, President Kennedy issued Executive Order 10925, which introduced the term "affirmative action" and created the Equal Opportunity Employment Commission.

In April, Governor Elmer Anderson signed the Minnesota Fair Housing Law, which was witnessed by four of its strongest advocates, Denzil Carty, Zetta Feder, Josie Johnson and Richardson Okie, who lobbied hard for its passage. The bill passed the Senate by only a six-vote margin, but had a comfortable majority in the House and became law on December 31, 1962.

In May, Richard Fox, Assistant Director of the Minnesota FEPC was appointed Special Assistant to the Deputy Assistant Secretary of Personnel for the U.S. State Department. He was replaced by James C. McDonald from the St. Paul Urban League.

In June, Father Carty was given a testimonial dinner by the members of his parish for his eleven years as their rector. At the Ceremony, Governor Orville Freeman declared June 11th as "Father Carty Sunday," Stephen Fligelman, the chairman of the Civil Rights Committee of the State NAACP, spoke of Carty's presidency as being a, "combination of gentility and silent strength." He called Carty, "tolerant in fighting intolerance," and noted that Carty appeared before countless committees and interracial groups in his effort to win support for his bill.

In August, President Kennedy appointed James P. Parsons, as the first African-American Federal District Judge ever to serve in the continental United States.[8]

Also that month, Allie Mae Hampton, who was active in the labor movement for almost a decade as president of the BSCP Ladies Auxiliary, became the newly elected president of the St. Paul NAACP. She along with Medgar Evers and nine other delegates, met with President Kennedy to seek his support for additional civil rights legislation.

That month, Carl Rowan, an African-American staff writer for the Minneapolis Star and Tribune turned down an invitation to speak at Oberlin's Commencement ceremonies because the school had expelled 14 students for participating as Freedom Riders in Jackson, Mississippi.

That fall, the Southern Regional Council announced that the sit-in movement was now in 20 states and 100 southern cities. At least 70,000 African-Americans and whites had participated in the movement and the council had estimated that 3,600 had been arrested and at least 141 students and 58 faculty members had been expelled by college authorities. The council also reported that 108 southern and border cities had been desegregated as a result of the sit-ins.

In September, the Boyinton v. Virginia decision, in favor of integrating interstate transportation facilities, which had previously been won by Thurgood Marshall in a 7–2 decision before the U.S. Supreme Court, was reaffirmed by the unanimous decision of the Court in Garner v. Louisiana, which Marshall argued on the basis of the Fourteenth Amendment.[9]

In October, James McDonald became only the second African-American to be administrative head of a state FEPC when Governor Anderson named him to head the state's commission.

In November, Macalester College historian Earl Spangler published his, *The Negro in Minnesota*, and Minnesota became the third state to publish a history of its black citizens.

Also that month, the Twin City Council of Clubs named Allie Mae Hampton "President of the Year."

In January 1962, at the Twin Cities Annual Hot Stoved League Baseball Banquet, Twins players, Early Battey and Lennie Green got up and walked out of the dinner after sportswriter Rosy Ryan told a story in which he characterized African-American people as, "blackbirds." D.J. Leary of KDWB defended their actions.[10]

The following month, attorney Joseph Robbie, accepted the case of African-American St. Paulite Robert H. Robinson, who had been incarcerated from June 6, 1959 to January 22, 1960 before going to trial. At his trial, he was acquitted of a burglary charge, but was rearrested again on May 1960 on the grounds that he had committed an additional offense at the same time of his original offense. He was again acquitted of the alleged offense, but was rearrested a third time on September 22, 1961, on the same charge from which he had formerly been acquitted. He was forced to spend eight more months in jail until April 1962 despite the fact that there had been no convictions. Robbie told Robinson that he should consider bringing suit against the City of St. Paul for unlawful arrest.[11]

In March, Newman strenuously objected in an editorial to a provision in a proposed state law which would require new state residents to provide proof of their voter qualifications from the precinct clerks of the former state or county from which they came. After reading Newman's editorial, Douglas Head, the author of the bill in question, H.R. 483, agreed to eliminate the provision after Newman informed him of the adverse effect it would have on African-Americans who came from states with barriers against African-American voters.

In April, the St. Paul Teachers Federation Local #28 objected to the appearance of General Electric spokesman Ronald Reagan's appearance at a Central High School Assembly on the grounds that he was merely, "a right-wing propagandist whose theme of, 'more guns, less butter and fewer taxes,' was a one-sided ideology." Newman congratulated the teachers on their spirited opposition. Later he noted in his editorial that it was much ado about nothing as Reagan, "was merely a harmless hero of the fruitcake fringe and had the crack-pottiest ideas now floating around in the political soup." Newman contended that if the school board persisted in allowing him to speak the least they could do was to present a, "capable literate and well-spoken leader of the opposite persuasion to rebut Reagan's right-wing ideology."[12]

That spring, when President Kennedy named Charles Moore, of Collinsville, Illinois to the post of U.S. Marshall, he became only the second African-American in history to serve in that capacity since the appointment of Frederick Douglass in 1877.

In May, Gunnar Myrdal, the author of *The American Dilemma*, suggested that "the progress of African-Americans since 1942 had been largely due to the 'activism of the civil rights movement which had stirred the conscience of whites...growing affluence had encouraged more mingling and less interest in keeping others down…as well as an increase in similarity in the likes and dislikes of an enlarging black and white middle class.'"

That summer, when States Human Rights Executive Director James McDonald accompanied Governor Anderson to the Governors Conference in Hershey, Pennsylvania, he was surprised to find that he was the only African-American professional staff person in attendance. The other African Americans were domestic servants – waiters, drivers and bellhops. When he and Governors Anderson and Rockefeller offered a strong civil rights resolution to the conference, it was defeated by southern governors.

In November, the Reverend Edward Grzeskowiak, the pastor of St. Peter Claver Catholic Church, became the new spiritual advisor for the Twin City Catholic Interracial Council. He served as moderator for the group's Fourth Annual Human Rights Workshop at the College of St. Catherine. The theme of the workshop was, "Improving Race Relations of Parish Youth." The workshop commended Louisiana's Archbishop Joseph Rummel, for his excommunication of three segregationists who were opposing his order to integrate the New Orleans Parish Schools.

Later that month, Cecil Newman, who had been the person who had suggested to Governor Thye the formation of an Interracial Commission in 1943, was finally asked to serve on the States' Human Rights Commission after having been passed over for almost two decades.

In April 1963, in the State Capitol rotunda, Father Carty led 300 people in prayer for the passage of a National Civil Rights Bill and urged them to write letters to their congressmen to encourage them to increase their efforts to secure adoption. He was joined in prayer by both Father Grzeskowiak and Rabbi Jerrold Goldstein. Near the end of that month, Governor Karl Rolvaag asked the legislature to grant his Interracial Commission the power to terminate public contracts that included discrimination and to eliminate discrimination in state job training programs and hiring practices.[13]

In May, Flora Galloway, a freshman at North Carolina A & T School of Nursing, picketed the local McDonald's Restaurant until it opened its doors to African-American customers later in the month.[14]

In June, for the first time in the nation's history, an American president publicly admitted that segregation was immoral. In a radio-TV address, President Kennedy said, "It was time for the Congress to act as segregation is morally wrong and that individual states as well as local bodies of government should also act as we should in all of our daily lives, to end it!"

In August, activists Denzil Carty, the Reverend Kneely Williams, Donald Smith, Robert Lippert and Connie Price led the St. Paul delegation in the largest African-American protest march in the nation's history. On the Mall, 250,000 citizens assembled and demanded legislation to end discrimination in education, housing and employment.

Two days, after King's historic, "I Have a Dream," speech, W.E.B. DuBois died in Accra, Ghana, at the age of 95. His legacy included 2,377 articles, books and pamphlets, which gave him the distinction of having been America's most prolific African-American literary genius. His writing covered almost every conceivable political, sociological and historical topic on African-Americans, a term which he argued when addressing Americans whose ancestors came from Africa. He was not only a brilliant and powerful writer, but also a humanistic intellectual who felt deeply for his people and after his death was sorely missed by most.

That fall, Arthur McWatt, president of the Twin City Catholic Interracial Council, accompanied Branches Editor James Leadon to a civil rights workshop in Chicago sponsored by the National Conference for Interracial Justice. After two days of workshops they returned home but left soon after for Washington D.C. to lobby congressmen for the passage of a civil rights legislation. While there they visited the offices of Representative Karth and Fraser and told them of their concerns.

On November 22nd, John Fitzgerald Kennedy was assassinated in Dallas, Texas, which was depressing to civil rights supporters. A Gallup Poll taken after his death showed a definite drop in expectations by both whites and African-Americans in their hopes for the future success of civil rights programs.

In 1964, Martin Luther King became the first African-American to be named, "Man of the Year," by Time magazine.

Carl Rowan, who had been serving as Ambassador to Finland the past year, was picked by President Johnson to be Director of the U.S. Information Agency, thus becoming the first African-American to attend National Security Council meetings on a routine basis.

Perhaps the most significant U.S. Supreme Court ruling that year was in the Griffin v. County School Board (U.S. 218, 234), which ended the desegregation doctrine of "all deliberate speed" and its unequivocal ruling that separate school systems in southern states must be merged. It served to buttress the 6–36-3 Baker v. Carr "One Man, One Vote decision" of the previous year that had declared reapportionment, "a basic constitutional right" and subsequently changed biracial politics and reapportionment in 36 states by 1970.

Katie McWatt was appointed in 1963 by Mayor George Vavoulis to act as chairperson of the St. Paul Minority Housing Committee. The Committee was charged with examining problems that affected African-Americans in their search for housing. The group held public hearings in the community so that those who had ideas, information or personal experiences could be heard. The recommendation of the Committee was for the passage of a fair housing ordinance by the St. Paul City Council. A Fair Housing Ordinance was passed later which gave responsibility for enforcement to the St. Paul Civil and Human Rights Department.

In March 1964, civil rights activists, Reverend Denzil Carty, Kwame McDonald, Alpha Adkins convinced Katie McWatt to run for a seat on the St. Paul City Council. There had never been an African-American on the Council in the history of the City. Her experience as an advocate for improved educational opportunities, the hiring of more African-American school staff, lobbyist for non-discrimination in housing, employment of African-Americans in the building trades and a dedication to social justice were critical issues for McWatt.[15]

Katie McWatt

She had the support of the local neighborhood organizations, the North Central Voters League, and was endorsed by the Democratic Farmer Labor Party (DFL). Her grounding in government process came from her period working with the St. Paul League of Women Voters. She helped organize for the group and also encouraged them to place human rights on their agenda.

McWatt attended numerous coffee parties; door knocked in every ward and had volunteers staff the Katie For Council office located at the intersection of University and Rice Street. McWatt proved to be an excellent campaigner with a good command of the issues, extraordinary energy and a good memory for names and faces. Her husband Arthur and four children Timothy, Stacy, Christopher and Lynn supported her during this busy period.

McWatt's primary campaign showed that she captured 74 percent of Summit University, 84 percent of her precinct and 32 percent of the City. She became the first African-American woman to win a St. Paul City Council Primary and her name was placed on the general election ballot. She made a very strong showing and received 38,487 votes in the at-large citywide election; but she lost by less than 2000 votes.

CHAPTER NINE 1960 – 1969

On June 10th, Editor Newman watched intently from his seat in the Senate Gallery as the body voted 71 to 29 to approve a motion for cloture after having endured a 75-day filibuster against the Civil Rights bill by southern Senators. The majority whip, Senator Humphrey, felt by 11 a.m. that he had the required votes and rose to address the Senate. He spoke in a serious and solemn tone as he said, "The Constitution of our great nation is on trial here today." He went on to urge the Senate to make 1964 a "Freedom Year."

Humphrey had worked hard during the spring, by having a long series of meetings with African-American civil rights leaders, including Clarence Mitchell, the former Executive Director of the St. Paul Urban League, who had served since 1950 as the Director of the Washington Bureau of the NAACP. Some years later, he dubbed him "the 101st Senator of the U.S. Congress," as a man who had worked tirelessly to persuade both undecided Senators, as well as Representatives to support civil rights legislation. The bill's passage was finally assured when Senate Majority Leader Mike Mansfield gained the support of Senate Minority Leader Everett Dirkson and Bourke Hickenlooper and cloture was finally achieved for only the sixth time in history.

After the cloture vote, Mitchell, who never forgot the unfinished business that remained, instead of joining his proponents in celebration, quietly walked Senator Russell back to his Senate office.[16] The final vote on the bill was 73–27 after 83 days of debate. Senator Goldwater, Russell and five other Republicans and twenty Democrats voted against the bill's passage. On June 30th, the House bill was approved by a 289-126 vote and three hours later, using 72 pens, President Lyndon Johnson, signed the bill into law.

In the middle of July, Stephen Maxwell was appointed St. Paul's first African-American Corporate Counsel.[17]

In August, the St. Paul City Council adopted a new Human Rights Ordinance by a unanimous vote which forbade discrimination in housing, public services and education.

In October, Dr. Charles Williams was enrolled in the Order of the Knights of Saint Gregory. As an African-American dentist in St. Paul, he suddenly found himself being courted by the local Knights of Columbus, who had turned him down when he had previously applied. They told him they had recently voted to abolish the rule that barred African-Americans for the past 82 years, but Williams quietly informed them he was no longer interested in becoming a member of their group.

That summer, the Minnesota delegation at the Democratic convention, which was on the record as supporting the seating of the Mississippi Freedom Democratic Delegation (MFDD), was embarrassed and dismayed when they discovered that Attorney-General Mondale, in his role as Chairman of the Convention's Credential Sub-Committee, had at the urging of Senator Humphrey, agreed to bar the MFDD delegation from being seated. Mondale, Humphrey and Walter Reuther carried out Johnson's attempt to prevent a walk-out of southern delegates by compromising the seating of the MFDD. Nevertheless, the southern delegates walked out later in the preceedings.[18] It also resulted in a subsequent crisis of confidence within the Democratic party and a disillusionment with liberals throughout the rank and file of the civil rights movement. The deed insured Humphrey appointment as Vice-President and Mondale an early selection to the U.S. Senate, but it undoubtedly hurt them both in their future bids for the Presidency.

Early in January 1965, Donald Lewis placed picket lines around the administration building of the St. Paul Public Schools in an attempt to energize St. Paul school officials to further desegregate the city's schools and warned them that he was preparing a lawsuit to challenge them.

In February, black nationalist Malcolm X began to sense that his life was in jeopardy when the U.S. State Department refused to grant him a visa to visit France.[19] On February 21st, he was murdered by members of a dissenting Muslim cell in New York, led by Louis Farrakhan. Malcolm thus joined the martyred ranks of extraordinary black uncompromising heroes such as David Walker, Martin Delaney, Henry Highland Garnett, William Monroe Trotter, Marcus Garvey and Paul Robeson, all of whom made unequivocal demands for full civil rights for America's African-Americans.

In March, after taking part in an orderly demonstration in St. Paul, Martin Luther King was chastised by the *St. Paul Pioneer Press*, "to try an act more statesmanlike rather than like the leader of a mob." After the paper accused him of "upsetting law and order in our town," he led a demonstration in St. Paul.[20]

That spring, Father James Flahaven, an advisor to the Catholic Interracial Council, organized a fund to help pay the expenses of local civil rights workers in the South. The first recipient was Leonard N. Mitchell, of St. Paul, who was doing voter registration in Selma, under SNCC's, "One Man, One Vote," slogan. Father Gryeskowiak announced that the Council was also granting 13 more scholarships for minority students to attend Catholic High Schools in the Twin City areas, which brought the total to 23 since the program began in 1960.

That summer, Leonard Carter, of St. Paul, was promoted to NAACP West Coast Regional Director. His promotion coincided with the passage of the Voting Rights Law, which once again required the invoking of cloture in the U.S. Senate. After a 24-day debate, the vote was 77–19. Within three months of its passage, over 100,000 African-Americans were able to vote for the first time. The new law suspended the use of literacy tests, and gave pre-clearance powers to Attorney-General Nicholas Katzenback, whose voting registrars had the right to challenge voter qualifying tests and to take actions against local election boards. Unlike the weak enforcement provisions under the Civil Rights Laws of 1957 and 1960, this law was stronger and the Justice Department was more assertive in its enforcement.

In a speech on June 4th, President Johnson perhaps laid the philosophical basis of affirmative action when he informed his listeners, "You do not wipe away the scars of centuries of saying now you're free to go where you want and do as you desire and choose the leaders you please. You do not take a person who for years has been hobbled by chains and liberate them and bring them to the starting line of a race and say you're free to compete with others. Negroes have been trapped in gateless poverty, they lack training and skills and have been shut in slums without decent medical care. We are trying to attack those evils!"[21]

In August, the Twin City Council of Churches honored Sam Scheiner, the Executive Director of the Jewish Community Relations Council, for his advocacy in organizing 37 clubs in St. Paul to work together for civil rights through collective fundraising and statewide lobbying of the legislature.

Mrs. Toni Lang, a white housewife from West St. Paul, was also presented with the J.F.K. Award for her dedication to civil rights in sheltering some African-American citizens who had escaped from Greenwood, Mississippi and for her participation in the Selma March. She had a cross burned on her lawn and received threatening phone calls that fall.[22]

In February 1966, Walter Mondale and Eugene McCarthy joined 18 colleagues to sponsor a bill, which would prosecute any person who attacked or killed a civil rights worker in the South. Representative Donald Fraser and Joseph Karth introduced the measure in the House and President Johnson, at the urging of Vice-President Humphrey, included it in the third civil rights bill he sent to the Congress. In the Senate, Senator McCarthy commented on the bill saying, "The origin of civil rights does not come from the Constitution or any document. They arise from human needs which we discover in our reflections on human nature within our society. From those reflections and observations, we come to accept the fact that certain needs are of such importance that they take on the character of human rights. Then it becomes the responsibility and the duty of a society to grant those human rights protection and thus they become civil rights."[23]

In March, the U.S. Supreme Court outlawed the Poll Tax for all elections which complemented the Twenty-Fourth Amendment, which had barred them in federal elections. That spring, when southern African-Americans learned that Edward W. Brooke had been elected a U.S. Senator in Massachusetts, that Percy Sutton had been elected Borough President of Manhattan and that African-American mayors had been elected in Flint, Michigan, and Springfield, Ohio, some of them began to sing a ditty in their churches which said;

"If you miss me in the white folks' kitchen,
And you can't find me no where,
Come on over to the courthouse,
I'll be clerkin' over there,
If you miss me on the paperwood track,
And can't find me no where,
Come on over to Camden,
I'm the mayor over there."

In May, the St. Paul NAACP, threatened to bring suit against the St. Paul School Board if they did not immediately remove the classrooms from the Maxfield Elementary School gymnasium and allow their students to use it as a recreational unit as it was intended.

In June, Judge Otis Godfrey spoke out against the proposed extension of Ramsey Junior High School's boundaries and against the fall integration of Linwood Elementary School graduates with those from Maxfield and J. J. Hill Elementary Schools. He said those schools had too high a degree of social disorder, juvenile delinquency, transiency and crime.[24]

In July, the St. Paul civil rights community was saddened by the death of Jonas G. Schwartz, who had been one of the major advocates in getting federal fair employment legislation passed and also one of the founders of the Minnesota United Negro College Fund.

Also in July, St. Paul's North Central Voters League received a $326,000 grant from the federal government to aid families in need. They established an adult education program and a Headstart program for 3–6 year olds. In addition, it presented a series of lectures on family problems, child-rearing and family.

In November, African-American Democrats won 133 legislative seats in 21 states, re-elected six congressmen, and increased the seats in state governments by 60. Edward Brooke became the first African-American U.S. Senator since Reconstruction.[25]

Early in 1967, when Representative Karth returned to Minnesota to address his Fourth District constituency, African-American civil rights activists, Denzil Carty, Urban League Board Chairman Lonnie Adkins, Community Service Director Katie McWatt and North Central Voter League President, Ray Hill quietly rose and walked out in protest for his vote to exclude Adam Clayton Powell from the 90th Congress.

In February, Clarence Mitchell III, who was born in St. Paul during the time his father was Executive Secretary of the local Urban League, was sworn in as the youngest State senator in Maryland's history. He had previously served as a State Representative for four years.

In April, the Minnesota Council for Civil and Human Rights, under the leadership of Richard Sykes, sent out literature to over 3,000 supporters to alert them to the expanded legislation on fair housing. Reverend Carty, Katie McWatt, Josie Johnson and Douglas Head were lobbying for Representative Fred Norton's bill, which put 70 percent of the state's homes under its provisions. It covered all homes except those which were owner-occupied, duplexes and rooming houses. With the help of Gary Flakne, the bill finally reached Governor Harold LeVander, who signed it into law.[26]

In June, President Johnson named Thurgood Marshall to the Supreme Court. He was confirmed on August 30th and became the country's first African-American Justice. On the 12th of that month,

Justice Warren wrote for a unanimous Court in Loving v. Virginia that its state law punishing persons who entered into interracial marriage violated both the due process and equal protection clauses of the Fourteenth Amendment.

In July, Governor LeVander appointed Stephen Maxwell to the St. Paul Municipal bench. He was the second African-American to be appointed in the state and the only one serving since the defeat of L. Howard Bennet.

Also that month, a 100-year-old tradition was broken when the Northern Pacific Railroad promoted Pullman porter George Young to the position of conductor. Government deregulation legislation forced the Pullman Company to separate its sleeping car services from its car-building operations and the company decided to sell its car services to various railroads.

In August, Janabelle Taylor became the first African-American and the only woman appointed to the state's first Metropolitan Council by Governor Harold LeVander.

In October, Representative Karth announced that the Midwest Research Council had found Minnesota to be the second among the 50 states in the categories of fairness in voting practices, in office-holding, employment, in the dissemination of justice and in according minorities access to education.[27]

The year ended with St. Paul Mayor Thomas Byrnes appointing Louis Ervin as Executive Director of the Department of Human Rights.

In February 1968, NAACP President Bradford Benner met with federal compliance officers of the Equal Economic Opportunity Commission (EEOC) and Northwest Airline officials in an attempt to resolve charges brought by African-American stewardesses Loretta Miller and Irene Gardner. Both claimed they had been made victims of racial slurs and acts of harassment while on duty. After a series of meetings with NAACP officers, a new policy was established by the Airline and their grievances were resolved.[28]

Also that month, U.S. Senator Walter Mondale joined Senator Edward Brooks in sponsoring S.R. 1358, a Fair Housing Bill, which dealt with the sale and rental of property. A similar bill was introduced in the House the following month. For only the eighth time in Senate history though the third time in the past four years, the U.S. Senate voted cloture 65 to 32, with 41 Democrats and 24 Republicans voting in favor of it. The bill not only banned racial discrimination in 80 percent of the nation's housing, but also made it a crime to harass or intimidate civil rights workers or to cross state lines to incite a riot.[29]

In March, Reverend Martin Luther King, Jr. announced plans for a Poor Peoples March on Washington, which would be made up of an army of poor whites, African-Americans and Hispanics that would convene in Washington D.C. on April 20th.

After his assassination on April 4th, 15,000 mourners marched in St. Paul in his memory. The 39- year-old Baptist preacher and Nobel Prize recipient had been the country's most effective civil rights warrior and had inspired millions with his Christian appeal. His philosophy was best expressed by his sage comment that, "It is true that morality cannot be legislated, but behavior can be regulated. The law may not make a man love me, but it may keep him from lynching me!" His concept of non-violence was accepted by millions of Americans for over a decade. After his civil and voting rights victories, his followers had forced him to broaden his concerns and radicalize his message and the racist backlash had resulted in creating an atmosphere which resulted in his assassination in Memphis, Tennessee.

His death caused a nationwide conflagration of African-American rage that swept the nation and resulted in the death of 46 people, the injury of at least 2,500, the incarceration of over 28,000 and property damage estimated at more that $50 million.[30]

CHAPTER NINE 1960 – 1969

In June, Architect Frank M. Smith died. He had been a past president of the local NAACP and a passionate advocate of fair housing and fought racial discrimination wherever he found it.

Also, the U.S. Supreme Court, in a 7–2 decision, extended their earlier ruling on housing to, "prohibit racial discrimination in the sale and rental of all properties including units containing fewer than five families, which had been exempted in the earlier law."[31]

In July, St. Paulite, Lou House was appointed Producer-Director of National Educational Television's (NET) new program, Black Journal.

That summer, civil rights activists Eloise Adams and Katie McWatt both filed to run for District House Seat 46B in the upcoming election.

That fall, Editor Newman concluded that his use of the term "Black" failed the test of exclusivity and that "Afro-Americans" was equally deficient as whites and Arabs from Africa could also be so designated if they simply became naturalized American citizens. He thus concurred that DuBois' term of African-American best suited Americans of African descent, just as Mexican-Americans, Japanese-Americans, Chinese-Americans and Native-Americans were equally suitable.

In September, the primary vote totals in 46B were tabulated and white candidate Roy Ryan received 1,241 while Katie McWatt received 968 and Eloise Adams only 434. In the general election, later that month, Mrs. McWatt lost by just under five hundred votes.

In October, after vandals had set fire to the home of Mr. and Mrs. John McKinney, police suspected racial bigotry. The McKinney's had saved up for 17 years to move out of the ghetto and two previous arson attempts had been aborted when the walls had failed to ignite. The following days neighbors and friends gathered and volunteered to repair the damage.

That month, when the Reverend Carty appeared before the St. Paul Urban Coalition, he was asked why more African-Americans were not taking advantage of their job offers. They were disturbed because the jobs that the National Association of Businesses were offering were not being actively sought. Carty told them that they shouldn't expect immediate responses from people who have had doors closed in their faces for over 300 years. "Certainly," he said, "motivation is lessened so you must spend more time and money to re-open them. You cannot merely advertise these jobs, but you must send people into these communities who will reach out to those who have been neglected and so long denied."

In November, Shirley Chisholm, of the Bedford-Stuyvesant section of Brooklyn became the first African-American woman ever elected to the U.S. House of Representatives when she defeated James Farmer in the 12th Congressional District, while Richard Nixon eked out a victory over Vice-President Hubert Humphrey by less that one vote per precinct.[32]

At the end of the year, the Census Bureau reported that 3,072,000 African-Americans were now registered to vote in the South and 51.4 percent of them had voted in 1968. It also reported that there were now 11 African-American federal judges, 79 state representatives, 18 state senators, and seven mayors. Since the enactment of the Voting Rights Law in 1965, there had been 385 public officials elected in state governments in the South and 1,702 African-Americans who held either elective or appointive positions in municipal and county governments.[33]

Early in 1969, Frank Kent, the newly appointed Commissioner of the Minnesota Human Rights Department, announced an agreement had been reached with Paper Calmenson to increase the recruitment of African-American employees under a new program called, "Project Equal Opportunity."

Also that spring, Katie McWatt, the Associate Director of Community Services, had "Know Your Rights" cards distributed to residents of the Summit-University community, which listed Kenneth

Griswold, Douglas Hall, and four other attorneys who had volunteered to help those stopped or held by police officers.

That summer, Richard Radman, the Secretary of the St.Paul Trades and Labor Assembly, perhaps by accident revealed his true feeling at an Assembly meeting when he commented that, "We think our contractors should hire minority workers during those times when many jobs are available…but three or four months from now when maybe 30 or 40 percent of our membership is not working we certainly don't want our contractors recruiting these new people for jobs, when our long-time union members are idle."

In July, Minnesota Mining and Manufacturing presented Rust College, of Holly Springs, Mississippi, with a $500,000 grant to establish a micro-film research center with materials on African-American history and culture. Also that month the Hill Foundation in St. Paul, also offered a $300,000 grant to United Negro College Fund members to sponsor workshops and seminars for librarians and media instructors on their campuses.[34]

During the first part of the month, civil rights activists, Executive Director Lawrence Borom of the St. Paul Urban League, Associate Director Katie McWatt, Alpha Adkins, James Shelton, Gladys Robinson, Evan Anderson, Odessa Bond, Reginald Harris and Marlene Johnson climbed into a sewer excavation on Dayton Avenue near Oxford Street. Marlene Johnson, who was later elected Lieutenant Governor of the state, stated that they were protesting the lack of minority workers being employed on city work projects in the Summit-University community. They

Odessa Bond

were directed to leave the excavation. They refused and they were arrested and taken to jail and booked for disorderly conduct. The demonstration convinced Mayor Byrne to meet with Human Rights Director Don Lewis and together they drew up measures that would increase the number of minority workers in the future. Civil rights attorneys Donald Heffernan and Ken Tilson had the groups' criminal charges dismissed.[35]

In September, Urban League attorneys filed suit on behalf of Lawrence Borom, Reginald Harris, Nick Castilla and the Citizens of St. Paul, "to enjoin the City of St. Paul from contracting with any firms that discriminated against minority persons. It also asked that the City be enjoined from disbursing any further funds to such contractors or employers who discriminate. Finally, it asked the court to compel the City to institute a program of affirmative action to insure that those with whom it contracts with in the future have a program of hiring minorities in place."

That fall, the ladies of the St. Paul American Legion Auxiliary refused to send African-American Regina Hicks, the duly elected governor of Girls State to the nation's capitol unless she promised to adhere to a set of conservative political positions to which they prescribed. Regina was adamant about maintaining her own beliefs and after the Reverend Denzil Carty intervened, was allowed to maintain her integrity while in attendance.[36]

In November, a committee headed by Associate Director Katie McWatt met with Superintendent William McRae of St. Cloud Reformatory to discuss problems concerning their inmates. Some of them had complained to the Urban League of unjust and cruel treatment because of having, "a poor orientation toward middle-class values," despite the fact that few of them came from the middle class. As a result of the meeting, a permanent committee was formed which included Katie McWatt, Harry Davis, Syl Davis, Bobby Hickman, Connie Price, Mahmoud El-Kati and Raymond Johnson, which continued to meet throughout the 1970s.

CHAPTER NINE 1960 – 1969

The year ended with former St. Paul Urban League Executive Director Clarence Mitchell being awarded the NAACP's coveted Spingarn Medal, "for his pivotal role in the enactment of civil rights legislation over the past three decades."

In the early 60s, African-Americans gave Kennedy the slender margin necessary to win and further empower the civil-rights movement. It started a Second American Revolution with sit-ins, freedom rides, the introduction of the term "Affirmative Action" in a 1961 Executive Order and the March on Washington.

Kennedy's assassination helped give impetus to the passage of both the Civil Rights and Voting Rights Bills. By the middle of the decade there was a move toward self-determination and empowerment through the Black Power and Muslim separatist movements led by Stokely Carmicheal and Malcolm X. Meanwhile, Johnson's Great Society became bogged down in the Quagmire of Vietnam.

The bright spots of the sixties included the election of Shirley Chisholm, the rise of the Mississippi Freedom Democratic Party, the emergence of Fannie Lou Hamer, the presentation of the Nobel Peace Prize to King, the 1964 Voting Rights Act and the 1968 Civil Rights Housing Law which forbade discrimination in 80 percent of the nation's housing and added protection to civil-rights workers.

By the end of the decade, the Silent Majority, which was made up of the oft-neglected West, the Goldwater-energized Bible-Belt, and northern conservative plutocrats gradually coalesced under Nixon's new policy of Benign Neglect toward ethnics of color.

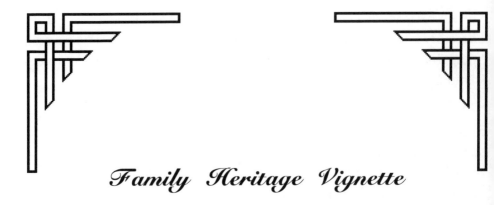

Family Heritage Vignette

Kathleen (Katie) Curry McWatt was born in Minneapolis to parents Mr. & Mrs. James Howard Curry (Helen Brady). Her sister Jean was eight years older. She graduated from the Minneapolis public schools. She went to the University of Minnesota where she earned her B.A. in Speech and went to the University of North Dakota for additional education in Counseling and Guidance. Her parents were born in Minnesota. Her mother was in the first graduating class from the newly built Minneapolis Central High School in 1914. Her father was a member of a large African American family who were born and raised in Hastings, Minnesota. He moved to Minneapolis, after graduating from Hastings High School, to become an automobile mechanic. He was the secretary of the African American chapter of the Masonic Lodge and an early member of St. Peter's AME Church.

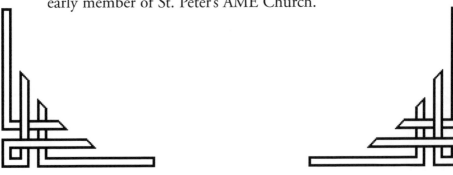

CHAPTER NINE BIBLIOGRAPHY

1. Bergman, Peter M. *The Negro in America*, p. 569.

2. *St. Paul Recorder*, 1 April 1960.

3. *St. Paul Recorder*, 6 May 1960.

4. Interview with Charles Rogers on August 2, 1979.

5. *St. Paul Recorder*, 21 August 1960.

6. Poinsett, Alex, *Walking With Presidents: Louis Martin and the Rise of Black Political Power*, Rowmand and Littlefield Publisher, New York, 1997, p.85.

7. *St. Paul Recorder*, 3 February 1961.

8. *St. Paul Recorder*, 8 August 1961.

9. Williams, Juan, *Thurgood Marshall: American Revolutionary*, Random House, N.Y.C., New York, 1997, p. 289.

10. *St. Paul Recorder*, 16 February 1962.

11. *ibid.*.

12. *St. Paul Recorder*, 10 May 1962.

13. *St. Paul Recorder,* 6 April 1963.

14. *St. Paul Recorder*, 30 May 1963.

15. *St. Paul Recorder*, 12 March 1964.

16. Humphrey, Hubert H., *The Education of a Public Man: My Life and Politics*, University of Minnesota Press, Minneapolis, MN, 1991, p. 211.

17. *St. Paul Recorder*, 16 July 1964.

18. Grant, Joanne, *Ella Baker: Freedom Bound*, John Wiley & Sons, New York, 1998, p. 171–175.

19. *St. Paul Recorder*, 25 February 1965.

20. *St. Paul Recorder*, 25 March 1965.

21. *St. Paul Recorder*, 14 August 1965.

22. Poinsett, Alex, *Walking With Presidents: Louis Martin and the Rise of Black Political Power*, pp. 152–153.

23. *St. Paul Recorder*, 17 February 1966.

24. *St. Paul Recorder*, 9 June 1966.

25. *St. Paul Recorder*, 19 November 1966.

26. *St. Paul Recorder*, 26 May 1967.

27. *St. Paul Recorder*, 12 October 1967.

28. *St. Paul Recorder*, 8 February 1968.

29. *St. Paul Recorder*, 15 February 1968.

30. Lewis, John, *Walking with the Wind: A Memoir of the Movement*, Simon and Schuster, New York City, N.Y., 1998, p. 389.

31. *Twin City Observer*, 27 June 1968.

32. Young, Andrew, *An Easy Burden: The Civil Rights Movement and the Transformation of America*, Harper Publishers, New York City, N.Y., 1996, p. 492.

33. Bergman, Peter M. *The Negro in America*, pp. 615-616.

34. *St. Paul Recorder*, 3 July 1969.

35. *St. Paul Dispatch-Pioneer Press*, 11 September 1969.

36. *St. Paul Recorder*, 16 October 1969.

Chapter Ten
1970 – 1979

"It is not enough to man the machinery of protest. Equally important today and twice as important tomorrow is participation in the responsibilities and opportunities of full citizenship in our democracy. This means moving, not only onto the picket line, but also the P.T.A. meeting, moving onto community councils, legislative committee rooms, commissions and boards to exercise our rights and ensure our fair share."

Whitney Young Jr., 1964

In January 1970, a survey conducted by St. Paul Civil Service Commissioner Lou McKenna found that in 14 of the 27 city agencies examined, there were no ethnics of color employed. No African-Americans were employed in the City Clerk's office, in the Bureau of Elections, in the Bureau of Records, nor in the City Comptroller's office, in the City Planning Office, in the Office of Civil Defense, in the Mayor's Purchasing Department or even in the Civil Service Department.[1]

Early that spring, Harry A Blackmun, a graduate of St. Paul's Mechanic Arts High School was named to a seat on the U.S. Supreme Court. He was promptly approved by the U.S. Senate. He was Nixon's third choice as his previous choices of Clement F. Haynesworth Jr. and G. Harold Carswell had been soundly rejected after concerted opposition from civil rights activists.

Later that spring the U.S. Census Bureau reported that over 1,500 African-Americans now held elective offices in the nation. There were 48 mayors, 575 city officials, 362 school board members, 168 state legislators, 114 state judges and 99 U.S. law enforcement officials. There was one African-American U.S. Senator and nine U.S. Representatives.

The only state-wide African-American official was Gerald A. Lamb, the State Treasurer of Connecticut.

In May, during the Second Annual Minnesota Human Rights Conference, Governor Harold LeVander replaced Human Rights Director Frank Kent with Conrad Balfour. Balfour had previously served as Assistant Deputy Director of the Twin City Opportunities Industrialization Center (TCOIC).

Later that month, Newman reported a school integration story, which reflected on the rate of progress that was being made in Mississippi. It was about School Superintendent E.G. Palmer of DeKalb High School in Kemper County, Mississippi, who contended that his school was "fully integrated." He contended this despite the fact that all 108 of his African-American 10th-graders drove to school on a segregated bus, all attended separate classes, and all ate their lunches in a separate study hall and all were taught by African-American staff. Their biology teacher, Miss Vera Kirkland told reporters, "The school is so segregated that we see whites only when we peek out our classroom curtains."[2]

That summer, civil rights activists throughout the country breathed a sigh of relief when President Nixon reluctantly signed a bill extending the Voting Rights Law through 1975 though the bill was weakened when Nixon extended its coverage to include both Puerto Ricans and Native Alaskans while not requesting any increase in funding.

In July, Elmer Childress became the first African-American candidate in Minnesota history to be endorsed for a statewide office by a major political party. He was chosen by the Democratic-Farmer-Labor Party as their candidate for Secretary of State. In the ensuing general election Childress ran against Bob Mattson Jr., whose father Robert Mattson had been Minnesota's State Treasurer for many years. Some Republican supporters deliberately gave the impression to voters that the son was really the father, which resulted in Childress receiving only 22,007 votes while the pseudo-father-son duo received 72,101.³

Also in July, the St. Paul Athletic Club's membership committee turned down Urban Coalition Director William O. White's application for membership. White had been a long-time secondary teacher in St. Paul as well as a recent graduate of the William Mitchell College of Law. He was finally accepted after agitators aroused the community and advocates negotiated a settlement.⁴

By the end of the year, the newly formed Joint Center of Political Studies reported that 665 new African-American office holders had been elected during the year. This included five new congressmen and it also noted that voter registration rolls had increased by over 200,000.

In January 1971, 12 Democratic African-American members of the U.S. House of Representatives formed the Congressional Black Caucus. It was chaired by Representative Charles Diggs Jr. of Detroit, Michigan, who was often called, "Mississippi's congressman-at-large", because of his avid support for voter registration programs in that state. Member John Conyers co-sponsored the Medicare bill and member William Clay became famous for modernizing Frederick L. McGhee's dictum that, "Blacks can have no permanent friends nor permanent enemies, only permanent interests." Another important member of this historic group was Representative Shirley Chisholm, who ran the following year for the Presidency of the United States and in the process registered hundreds of thousands of African-American voters. The entire Black Caucus boycotted President Nixon's State of the Union message because of his refusal to meet with them and respond to their "Petitions of Black Americans."

In February, Larry Borom resumed his duties from Katie McWatt, who had been Acting Director during his academic sabbatical. During his absence, McWatt had established a Legal Defense Fund, which was staffed by volunteers Alpha Adkins, Estyr Peake and the Reverend

Denzil Carty, who was its treasurer. The fund was to help combat the City Council's passage of the "Stop and Frisk" law and was to be used to help defend young African-American men who were challenged under this statute by city police officers and who did not have the means or knowledge to defend themselves.

Estyr Peake

In March, St. Paulites were saddened to hear that their former Urban League Director, Whitney Young, had died of a cerebral hemorrhage while swimming about 100 yards off the coast of Lagos, Nigeria. He had been there attending a meeting of African leaders and his body was returned to New York City where he had served as Executive Director since October 1, 1961. Over 6,000 mourners attended his service at Riverside Church.

That summer, Josie Johnson, civil rights activist, became the first African-American woman to be elected a Regent of the University of Minnesota. She was appointed by Governor Wendell Anderson and her confirmation was guided through the state Senate by DFL Majority Leader, Nicholas Coleman.

In June, the U.S. Supreme Court ruled unanimously that busing was a constitutionally acceptable method of desegregating the public schools while also choosing to unanimously overturn the draft-evasion conviction of Muhammad Ali.

In July, Donald Lewis, the Deputy Director of the St. Paul Human Rights Department, received the 1971, "Outstanding Service Award" from the International Association of Human Rights Agencies. He had helped

Josie Johnson

strengthen human rights in St. Paul by helping amend the current law to include prohibitions against sex discrimination. Penalties for violations could bring up to $300 in fines and 90 days in jail.[5]

That fall, the St. Paul Urban League announced that St. Paul now had 85 African-American classroom teachers, three counselor interns, seven social workers, one school psychologist and seven administrative interns.[6]

In October, Lonnie Adkins, a prominent African-American architect and civil rights activist, died while jogging. For six years, Lonnie had headed the St. Paul Urban League's Board of Directors and was a militant advocate for racial equality. He had helped form the first St. Paul Urban Coalition and served as its first vice-president. In 1965, he had also led the St. Paul delegation on the Selma-to-Montgomery March.

In December, according to the Minnesota Department of Education Guidelines, both Mechanic Arts Junior and Senior High Schools, Marshall Junior High School and Roosevelt Junior High School were segregated. Elementary schools that were victims of "white flight" were Hill, Maxfield, Roosevelt and Webster schools. The Board also set up a Human Relations component that was required to be taken before new teachers could receive certification to pass or to renew their licenses.[7]

In Washington D.C., there was a weakening of the civil rights movement when activists failed to stop the confirmation in the U.S. Senate of William H. Rehnquist to the U.S. Supreme Court. He had an anti-civil rights record including a habit of challenging African-American voters credentials in voting lines and who along with the newly appointed Justice Powell, inaugurated a new era of conservatism on the high court.[8]

In January 1972, U.S. Representative Shirley Chisholm (D-NY) continued her presidential campaign and after seven months and eleven primaries had garnered 28 delegates though her total would be 151.25 by convention time in July. She was accomplishing what no other female candidate had ever dared to do and she was doing it with a national office staff of three full-time people in Washington D.C. She continued to speak out on the issues of unmet social needs and remind Americans that their democracy was seriously flawed as long as class, gender, generation-gaps and race discrimination were allowed to be victims of Nixon's "Benign Neglect" policies toward minorities. "

In February, the St. Paul Urban League was successful in getting the St. Paul area office of the Department of Housing and Urban Development (HUD) to establish minimum requirements for employment in conjunction with the St. Paul Building and Construction Trades Council, the Minnesota State Building Trade Council and the Associated General Contractors of Minnesota. The four groups established a goal of 4 percent employment for all minorities of color on HUD-financed projects by 1975. The building trade unions also promised to integrate their membership by adding one percent each year for the next four years. This program would also include the hiring of minority apprentices and journeymen under Presidential Executive Order #11246.[9]

Former St. Paulite George Holland, who had served on the St. Paul Urban League Board from 1945–55, was now Deputy Assistant Secretary of Labor for Federal Contract Compliance and had been given the responsibility for the enforcement of this program to see that contractors practiced affirmative action in ensuring equal opportunity in employment practices, which Holland had not received during his early employment years with the Minnesota Milk Company.

In March, Adam Clayton Powell Jr., now a broken and ill man since his abuse by Congress, died. He had the distinction of being one of the first nationally significant African-American urban agitators, advocates and activists to institute well-organized, mass economic boycotts and marches, which successfully achieved civil rights reforms in the 1930s and discernible successes in the 1940s.

Also that month, President Nixon appointed Benjamin Hooks as the nation's first African-American Federal Communications Commissioner even though African-Americans in the country owned only 16 radio stations and no television stations.[10]

In April, the Reverend Denzil Carty was the recipient of the Ramsey County Bar Association's Liberty Bell Award for "his outstanding and significant contributions to law and to the community." He was the first African-American to receive the award.[11]

In May, after efforts by both Representative August Hawkins (D-CA) and Senator Hubert Humphrey, the army finally took steps to clear the record of Dorsie Willis, an African American from Minnesotan who had been one of the 167 soldiers of the 25th Infantry's 1st Battalion who had been summarily dishonorably discharged by President Theodore Roosevelt as a result of the Brownsville Incident in 1906. It concerned a group of 16 to 20 armed men who had ridden through the town on that August 13th firing from horseback which resulted in the death of a townsman. Though the soldiers of the 1st Battalion, 25th Infantry, had no horses and though the shell casings recovered after the incident did not come from any of the weapons issued to the 1st Battalion, they were discharged, "without honor from the army."[12]

In August, Captain James S. Griffin was appointed St. Paul's first African-American Deputy Chief of Police after having been first passed over by Chief Richard Rowan. Rowan chose to recommend to Mayor Cohen the appointment of William McCutcheon. This was done despite the fact that, "Griffin had received a 90.4 on the Deputy Chief examination while McCutcheon had received only an 89.6." By his actions, Rowan broke a 30-year precedent by giving preferential treatment and Griffin immediately filed a grievance with the civil service commission while receiving support from the Police Union. Griffin hired attorney Douglas Thompson to represent him.

Griffin had felt somewhat vindicated when Chief Rowan finally decided to add a Deputy Chief position to cover the north sector of the city and had told Mayor Cohen to have Griffin fill it. After the appointment, however, Chief Rowan continued to harass Griffin during his regularly held meetings of police stewards, union leaders and Deputy Chiefs and during subsequent absences, placed him in charge of the department only three times during Griffin's eleven-year tenure.[32]

President Stephen Seals of the St. Paul NAACP suggested it sounded like chicanery and pointed out that Griffin had eleven years more seniority than McCutcheon and should have been assigned a regular sector. He further noted that the actions simply, "created further suspicions toward the St. Paul Police Department and, "widened the gulf which already exists between them and our community. If a black man cannot be promoted to a position by finishing on top after an examination when will he ever be promoted? In the past, the hope of the black man going to the top of his profession was small. Now, it appears that this fact will remain intact."[13]

Also in August, Ron Jones, the Associate Director of the St. Paul Urban Coalition, announced that his firefighter tutorial program that had been instituted the previous year had produced seven candidates who had passed the firefighters exam, but only one had been hired.[14]

Later that month, Director Talmer Curry with the McGough Construction Company placed nine graduates of the St. Paul Urban League Education Apprenticeship Program (LEAP). They were carpenter apprentices and were each given a complete set of carpenter tools to start their new assignments.

In September, Executive Director Larry Borom began a selective buying campaign against General Mills because of their failure to practice fair employment practices. He told his board of directors that there was ample evidence of discrimination against both African-American men and women. He received support from the National Urban League office.

By November, the St. Paul Fire Department had a complement of only five African-American firemen out of a total force of 454. The Urban League filed a discrimination suit against the city, on behalf of six firefighter candidates, James Fowler, William Hall, Lawrence Walker, David Jackson, Verdea Webb and Vernon Cryer. They were all residents of St. Paul and they charged the St. Paul Fire Department with employment discrimination. Judge Edward Devitt was the presiding official.[15]

Also in November, pre-law student Bill McGee was beaten and kicked by St. Paul Police officers Thomas Fabio and David Ebert, until his body was a mass of bruises and welts and his face bloody. The officers claimed that McGee did not stop for a red light and tried to flee after he got out of his car. His parents, Earl and Anna McGee, of Rochester, filed a suit against Chief Rowan and Mayor Cohen.[16]

In December, Judge Devitt granted the seven firefighter applicants a permanent injunction against both the St. Paul Fire Department and the St. Paul Civil Service Commission. This prevented them from hiring any firefighters until they had developed new tests. The plaintiffs were represented by Attorneys Andrew Haines and Delores Grey were assisted by investigators, Edgar Pillow of the Urban League and Robert Harris, President of the Summit University Federation.[17]

In February 1973, Ted Allen, who co-authored the new St. Paul City Charter the previous summer, became the first African-American member of the St. Paul Charter Commission.

In March, Garth C. Reeves, the president of the National Newspaper Publishers Association (NNPA) and the editor-publisher of the Miami Times, noted in an editorial that according to Harvard researcher, Dr. Henry G. LaBrie, there had been 3,000 African-American newspapers published since John Russwurm's Freedom Journal had been published in September 1827. In 1972, 208 were still in publication. In 1973, there were only three African-American dailies still publishing. They were the Atlantic Daily World, the Chicago Daily Defender and the New York Daily Challenger. The weeklies still publishing which had been founded in the nineteenth century were the Philadelphia Tribune (1884), the Baltimore Afro-American (1892), The Houston Informer (1894), the Des Moines Bystander (1894) and the Indianapolis Recorder (1895).[18]

That summer, Dorsie Willis received $25,000 as the result of the efforts of Representative Donald Fraser and Senator Humphrey. Fraser had worked with Senator Humphrey in the conference committee on Willis' behalf. It served as a rather weak compensation for the 50 years Willis had spent shining shoes which he claimed was due in large part to this dishonorable discharge, which had made him ineligible to seek the civil service job to which he aspired. He also received a letter of apology from the Secretary of the Army.

That fall, Robert Patterson the Secretary of Local #516 of the Dining Car Employees Union, charged that Amtrak, which President Nixon had organized under the Regional Rail Re-Organization Act of 1973 was using "union-busting" tactics. Patterson claimed that the newly formed Amtrak, "had arbitrarily canceled union payroll deductions, had ignored union shop agreements, had cut wages and had introduced new work rules without either consulting or even communicating with Local #516." He also claimed that the Railroad Labor Act, which required collective bargaining, had been totally ignored by the Nixon administration's Labor Relations Board. He noted that though a large percentage of Amtrak employees lived in St. Paul, the company had failed to base any official in St. Paul to handle employee complaints or grievances. Employees unable to work had to notify Chicago six hours in advance. He also charged that Amtrak had canceled their employee health service contract and that employees had been told that if they wanted to keep their health coverage they would have to retain them on an individual basis. Amtrak went on to cancel all employee payroll deductions through their employees' credit union, and a great #516 tradition that had been organized in 1938 by Maceo Littlejohn, Hector Vassar, Maceo Finney and Robert Patterson was destroyed. St. Paul had been a junction at one time or another for 27 railroads and would now likely serve merely as a minor junction for Amtrak's northern transcontinental runs.[19]

At the end of the year, Lawrence Borom announced that the St. Paul Urban League during the past year had generated 3.5 million dollars in new contracts and business and had provided technical assistance and promotion to over 125 minority and majority business firms who aided minority business development. The League had also placed 185 apprentices through its State Highway Program and placed 218 On-the-Job trainees.[20]

In January 1974, Lawrence Borom accepted the position of National Director of Community Development with the National Urban League in New York City. While serving in St. Paul, Borom had expanded the league's community services in housing, education and legal assistance. He had been able to secure funds for a labor education program, for an on-the-job training program, a day care center, a street academy for drop-outs and those with learning disabilities, as well as an employment recruitment program for the Minnesota Highway Department. Under the initiative of Community Service Director Katie McWatt, the league had saved, relocated and rehabilitated ten homes, which, had been scheduled for demolition at the new Maxfield Elementary School site.

In April, Archie Givens, the state's first African-American millionaire, died suddenly of a heart attack. In the 1950s, his Tilsen Homes had provided the first breakthrough for new housing for African-Americans in 30 years. In the 1960s, he set up a philanthropic foundation that provided scholarships for African-American college students, which included students at Macalester College.[21]

In June, the U.S. Supreme Court, in Milliken v. Bradley denied the creation of metropolitan school integration by denying Detroit schools the right to merge with suburban schools by a 5–4 decision, which had repercussions for the next quarter of a century. Justice Marshall dissented and called the decision, "an emasculation of the Constitutional guarantees of equal opportunity in school desegregation."

After President Richard Nixon resigned in disgrace to avoid impeachment, President Ford became the first U.S. President to meet with the Congressional Black Caucus in seven years. The meeting was amiable, but afterwards, Ford announced to the press that he did not favor busing as a way to integrate American schools.

That fall, the Joint Center for Political Studies noted that, "America's Last Colony" Washington D.C. had finally been given Home Rule, which would take effect in the nation's capitol later that year.

In November, African-Americans in Mississippi elected fifteen state representatives and two state senators.[22]

In December, O. Donald Smith was the recipient of a HUD "Special Achievement Award." He received it because of his outstanding, "advocacy, imagination and innovative efforts in establishing career opportunities for African-American youth and for providing them employment over the past five years."[23]

Early in 1975, President Ford appointed William T. Coleman as his Secretary of Transportation, making him the first African-American Cabinet appointee of a Republican administration. He also appointed James B. Parsons of Chicago, as the first African-American Chief Judge of a federal district court.

That spring the Joint Center for Political Studies announced that 14 million African-Americans were now eligible to vote in America, just ten years after the passage of the Voting Rights bill.

Also that spring, civil rights supporter Senator Walter Mondale was able to modify Rule 22, which had been used for over a century to thwart civil rights legislation in the U.S. Senate. It had stymied the passage of over 200 anti-lynching bills alone. With the help of Republican James F. Pearson of Kansas, Mondale was able to fashion a truly historic Compromise Resolution, which diminished the number of votes needed to cut off debate from 67 to 60. It passed the Senate by a vote of 56–27.[24]

It was also about this time that firefighter Robert Harris was able to bring to fruition the efforts that he and eight other firefighters had started in 1972 over "the discriminatory nature of the city's firemen's examination." Attorney Andrew Haines had succeeded in proving, over a three year period, their contentions, that the firefighters tests were not job-related.[25] After winning the James Fowler Case, the St. Paul Fire Department agreed to set up a recruitment program for African-American candidates. Harris was named the program's director and he hired Bill Peterson and Dave Goodlow as physical training instructors and Bobby Hickman to do psychological testing. They succeeded in recruiting a class of over 200 candidates. After the physical fitness tests were completed the class had been pared to 110 and after further testing the number was down to less than one hundred. At the end of the training program, candidates Ora Peoples, James Fowler, Byron Brown, Roger Neal, Perry Harrison, Robert Mims, Gary Allen and James Logan were hired as city firefighters.

That fall, Donald Lewis, the Director of the St. Paul Department of Human Rights, announced that a new ordinance had been passed that would ensure equal opportunity for the disabled and handicapped persons working in St. Paul.

In October, Edgar Pillow, the Associate Director of Economic Development for the St. Paul Urban League, left the city to take another job. During his tenure, he had developed a man-power training program for corporations, installed minority management through his

Project Rehab, coordinated a survey of African-American employees in state government, was instrumental in bringing the suit against both the fire and police department of St. Paul to improve the fairness of their tests and had lobbied successfully for set-aside procurement legislation which the legislature had passed during their last legislative session.[26]

In November, with the help of Roscoe Hamby of the International Association of Firefighters, trainees, William Hall, Anthony J. Carter, John Foster, Ernest Coleman and James E. Smith were hired by the St. Paul Fire Department. This brought the total number of African-Americans to 13, which was almost four percent of the department's total.[27]

In January 1976, Jon Galloway of the State Equal Opportunity Commission (EEOC) charged that "it is becoming increasingly apparent to us that whenever we take a stand against either overt or covert discrimination between state departments, that complaints are being shuffled back and forth and are not being acted upon by either the department in question or the Department of Personnel. Galloway cited one case, in particular, which concerned the lack of African-American officers on the Minnesota Highway Patrol. He noted that there were only three officers of color, serving the department and all efforts to increase that number had been met with "total resistance." Suggestions continued to pass between departments without any seeming attempt to implement them. Some minority applicants who had successfully passed the written and oral tests were sometimes told that the job was no longer open. They were also further humiliated by being asked to enroll in a new "trainee program." This was done despite clear evidence that patrolmen's jobs were being filled by friends and relatives of patrolmen presently employed.[28]

Also that month, the Minnesota Supreme Court ruled, "calling a person a 'nigger' was a discriminatory offense punishable by punitive damages." January 23rd, the decision was handed down by Justice Fallon

Kelly who wrote, "A single act of discrimination, such as using a racial epithet, is all that is required for liability."[29]

On February 7th, Cecil Newman died at the age of 73. For over four decades, he had been an uncompromising advocate, leader and defender of the struggle for civil rights in the Twin Cities. Only four years after the death of J.Q. Adams, in 1923, he took over the reins of protest, when his first article in the *Herald* complained about police brutality in St. Paul. He kept his readers informed, aware, and involved by challenging, taunting, and confronting racism wherever he found it and was widely admired by all strata of society. Services were held at St. Peter's AME Church on February 10th and were attended by hundreds.

In May, Rosilyn Carroll became the first African-American woman ever elected to the St. Paul School Board. She was a graduate of Jamestown University in North Dakota and was endorsed by both the Minnesota DFL and MFT Local # 28.

In June, when Roy Wilkins was awarded an honorary Doctor of Laws Degree at the University of Minnesota, he noted in his address, that nationally the NAACP membership had doubled during the recent decades and that almost 4,000 African-Americans now filled elected offices throughout the nation though he tempered his remark with the fact that they still represented only two percent of the nation's total.

On July 12th, Representative Barbara Jordan (D-TX) became the first African-American to give a keynote address at a national convention of a major political party when she addressed the Democratic convention in New York City.

In August, when Roy Wilkins retired after leading the NAACP for over 22 years, Senator Walter Mondale, the Vice-President elect, had the *Recorder* editorial printed in the Congressional Record. It said, in part, "Roy Wilkins directed the largest civil rights organization in the world with both patience, dignity and with faith in the essential goodness of men and women of all races. Some said he was too quiet, too tolerant of others' prejudices and too much an evolutionist and not enough a revolutionist...but those who knew him well found that under his calm and polished manner was a crusader as dedicated as any in the country and a distinguished champion of racial justice."

That fall, Mayor George Latimer of St. Paul announced a new policy of evaluating contractors who were doing business with the city by determining how much effort they had made to improve job opportunities for persons of color.

In November, Jimmy Carter equaled Lyndon Johnson's vote total when he also received 94 percent of the 6.6 million votes of African-Americans in his bid for the Presidency against Ford.

In December, Hubert Humphrey lost his bid to become Majority Leader of the U.S. Senate to Senator Robert Byrd of West Virginia, which weakened Carter's presidency by denying his Vice-President, Walter Mondale, the guidance, stability and the wisdom of his mentor.

In January 1977, a new position was created for Senator Humphrey who was given the title of Deputy President Pro Tempore of the Senate. It was a post, which gave him an increase in pay, but left him off the first line of leadership and eased him into semi-retirement and again negatively impacted the civil rights movement. Asked by the press, if his demotion was the result of his chronic over-promising, Humphrey retorted, "You have to over-promise...the Sermon on the Mount was an over-promise, the Pledge of Allegiance was an over-promise. What you think you can do is only half of what you ought to try and do!"

In February, human rights advocate Katie McWatt was chosen, along with 24 other activists, to serve on the Minnesota Citizen's Review Commission. The purpose of the commission was to investigate and if necessary, expose, the efforts of the Federal Bureau of Investigation's CONINTELPRO division, which was suspected of trying to disestablish the Black Panthers and American Indian Movement (AIM).

That spring, St. Paul School Board members James Griffin, Rosilyn Carroll and others continued their efforts to protect the jobs of last-hired African-American, Native-American, Asian-American and Hispanic teachers. Despite the rumblings in the press of preferential treatment, the board finally took a courageous stand and reached the decision that all teachers of color would be exempt from layoffs. It was the only time in my memory that a public body took a stand that gave to persons of color privileges that whites have always, historically, taken for granted.[30]

That fall, African-American Commissioner of Personnel Richard Sessions, was accused of "giving too many minority females top jobs" by State Senator William McCutcheon, who chaired the Legislature's Audit Commission. Sessions responded by accusing McCutcheon of orchestrating a series of vicious McCarthy-type attacks on his character. McCutcheon then charged that Sessions had, "encouraged minority candidates to lie about their qualifications in order to get jobs." Sessions was vehement in his denial saying that the accusations were both, "untrue and unsupported by the facts." He told reporters that in order to protect the integrity of the agency, he intended to tender his resignation to the Governor.

It appeared Sessions' problems with State Senator McCutcheon began when he passed over the first-place test score of Stanley Rotegard, a close friend of Deputy Chief McCutcheon and a retired State Highway Patrolman, who was seeking the position of Security Chief for the Minnesota Zoological Gardens. He had been miffed when Sessions had offered the position to an African-American second-place finisher named Cedric Langham, who had been a correctional officer at Stillwater Prison.[31]

Ironically, McCutcheon had been the recipient of the same kind of treatment given Langham four years earlier when Chief Richard Rowan had given him the job of Chief over the first-place score of Captain James Griffin.

In December, Urban League Employment Director Talmadge Curry discovered that unscrupulous contractors were employing minority persons and women to "front" as owners to win contracts with the St. Paul School Board and exposed them through his investigation.[33]

After his death in January 1978, Hubert Humphrey was posthumously awarded the NAACP Walter White Award in St. Paul for his years of dedicated support for the cause of civil rights. His son, Hubert Humphrey II, accepted the award and said, "My dad believed and I believe that you never own anything in life; you only use it... you are a steward... he believed that the dream was always there before the reality."

A short time later, Allan P. Bakke, a pre-med student attempting to enter Medical School at the University of California, at Davis, made the first significant challenge of the concept of affirmative action when the U.S. Supreme Court majority ruled "that the sixteen seats set aside for African-Americans constituted a quota and had the effect of discriminating against qualified white applicants. It caused many government agencies to reevaluate their programs in favor of whites and resurrected the doctrine of "reverse discrimination," among those opposed to equal opportunity. Assistant Attorney General Drew Days did not help the cause of equal opportunity when he sent a memo to all federal agencies to "be more careful" in their enforcement of anti-discrimination laws.[34]

In March, the Brotherhood of Sleeping Car Porters (BSCP) merged with the Brotherhood of Railway and Airline Clerks. The porters now numbered less than a thousand members and felt the need to join the 250,000 member group to maintain bargaining power.

That summer, James "Baby" Eubanks, the Minister of the Interior of the Afro-American Brotherhood at Stillwater Prison, wrote the heads of the St. Paul and Minneapolis Urban Leagues. He wanted to thank them for allowing Katie McWatt, the St. Paul Director of Community Services to work with their group. In his letter, he said;

"Sister Katie McWatt has been a long-time consistent supporter of our Stillwater branch. Come hell or high water, Katie 'God bless her' has stuck with us over a period of seven years. Without her and the League's support our, 'row to hoe,' here at the prison would have been, without doubt, more difficult if not totally impossible. Last week we read that the St. Paul Urban League has launched its second annual membership fund drive with a goal of $30,000. Our Brotherhood would like to donate a $15 check to both the St. Paul and Minneapolis branches. As prisoners, we do not have much money, but part of what we do have we feel obligated to share with you…We believe that all Black people must wake up and begin to support their agencies who are waging the struggle for liberation, justice and equality. Enough said—Here's the Bread!"

In November, the St. Paul Urban League's On-the-Job Training Program signed a contract with Honeywell Avionics Division to train 17 persons in the clerical field in addition to the 14 who they had previously trained. Since the past October, their program placed 534 persons according to William Newsom, the League's Director, and those trained had a 93 percent retention rate since being assigned.[35]

In early 1979 in St. Paul, the spray-painting of Nazi symbols on the walls of Mount Zion Temple and the St. Paul Urban League prompted Mayor Latimer and the City Council to resolve to make a continuing effort to "ensure protection of democratic rights and constitutional liberties for all St. Paul citizens."

Also that month, Control Data set up a Fair-Break Educational Center at 704 University Avenue to help high school drop-outs. It was funded by a government-sponsored Comprehensive Employment and Training Act (CETA) and had 40 students enrolled. The Center offered remedial courses in reading language and math as well as a life management course and used the Control Data Plato computer-assisted education system. Many of the enrollees used the course to pass their high school equivalency GED tests while working half days at a Control Data assembly plant.

In May, the founder of the modern civil rights movement in the eyes of many, A. Philip Randolph, died in New York, at the age of 90. The Congressional Black Caucus honored his passing by setting up an "Action Alert" communication network to help their constituents exert additional pressure on their representatives to do a better job on civil rights matters.

In early June, the U.S. Supreme Court continued its campaign of weakening civil rights when it ruled in U.S. Steel v. Brian Weber that "private" employers could give special preference to African-Americans workers to help eliminate manifest racial imbalance in traditionally white jobs, but ignored the vast proportion of African-American workers who had "government" employers. Equal opportunity was also weakened in Weber v. Kaiser Aluminum and Chemical Corporation when the Court said that employers and unions could only establish "voluntary" programs to aid minorities in the areas of job discrimination rather than "legal."

Later that month, the *Recorder* pointed out that some of the traditional allies of the civil rights movement were now drawing away from the fight for economic equality. The editorial spoke of new antagonisms from the Anti-Defamation League and B'nai B'rith, who had previously positioned themselves on the cutting edge of civil rights reform, but were now aligned with Bakke. Regents of the University of California v. Bakke, 438 U.S. 265 (1978) was a landmark decision of the Supreme Court of the United States on affirmative action. The decision barred quota systems in college admissions, but affirmed the constitutionality of affirmative action programs giving equal access to minorities.

In September, the Anti-Defamation League had joined Bakke by filing, "a friend of the court" brief in the Bakke case, but went even further in the Fullerton v. Kreps case when the League called, "for an end to affirmative action and set aside programs." It continued a steady decline in civil rights programs as thousands of institutions began modifying and even redefining their commitment to affirmative action programs for ethnics of color and women.[36]

In October, the University of Minnesota had a 50 percent drop in minority student enrollment in the entering class and by the end of 1979 enrollment had dropped by 32 percent and had the lowest number of African-American students since the previous decade.[37]

In November, the St. Paul Urban Coalition reported increasing discrimination against people of color on the staff of the state's elected officials. The number had declined by over 40 percent with Governor Quie as well as six of the states' U.S. Representatives having none. It was also found that though 19 percent of the ethnics of color who worked for the state's constitutional officials held managerial positions, compared to only 14 percent for white employees, their salaries were 17 percent less than that of their white counterparts.[38]

Also that month, the vote to make Martin Luther King's birthday a national holiday fell short by six votes in the house of Representatives, 252–155, one of which was cast by Minnesota Representative William Frenzel who said, "This bill simply provides another day off for bureaucrats and will end up costing the nation $212 million dollars in lost wages and overtime."[39]

In December, after African-American Bill Wilson, former state commissioner of human rights, decided to run for the St. Paul City Council, Representative Fred Norton hosted a fundraiser for him at the St. Paul Labor Center. He told the gathered throng that Bill would bring, "intelligent, concerned, sensitive and strong leadership to our city government."

Looking back over the decade, St. Paulites could feel a sense of progress during the early part from the increase in human rights agencies and the introduction of affirmative action, the ending of the death sentence by the U.S. Supreme Court through the efforts of Justice Marshall, and the organization of 17 Congressional Black Caucus members. They could also take heart from the presidential campaign of Representative Chisholm, and the election of President Carter in 1976. While Presidents Nixon and Ford had appointed a total of six African-American Federal Judges during their tenure, Carter had appointed thirty-seven, with nine of them being placed on Courts of Appeal and six being the first black federal judges in the nation's history ever assigned to the South.[40]

One of Carter's white judicial appointees was Frank Johnson, the leader of the Fifth Circuits' "Four Horsemen of Civil Rights," whom Bill Moyers interviewed on his TV Journal program. He credited Johnson for being mainly responsible, during the previous quarter of century, for the desegregation of Alabama schools, their buses and terminals, their parks, museums, mental institutions, jails, prison, airports, and libraries. He noted also that Johnson had also drawn up the first court-ordered state legislative reapportionment in U.S. history, and had revolutionized the electoral and voter registration system by introducing his "Freezing Doctrine," which placed both blacks and whites under similar voting requirements. He abolished the state's poll tax even before Congress acted and became the first Judge in the history of the South to place women on juries.[41, 42]

But these gains were tempered by the Bakke decision, the Supreme Court's denial of metropolitan school integration, the reinstitution of the death penalty, and the machinations that took place in the appointment of the St. Paul Police Chief as well as the National Labor Relations Board's dismemberment of Dining Car Local #516. The St. Paul community also faced high unemployment, a rising crime rate and increasing white hostility.

CHAPTER TEN BIBLIOGRAPHY

1. *St. Paul Recorder*, 26 January 1970.

2. *St. Paul Recorder*, 28 May 1970.

3. *St. Paul Recorder*, 2 July 1970.

4. *St. Paul Recorder*, 9 July 1970.

5. *St. Paul Recorder*, 19 August 1971.

6. *St. Paul Recorder*, 30 September 1971.

7. *St. Paul Recorder*, 9 December 1971.

8. Williams, Juan, *Thurgood Marshall: American Revolutionary*, Random House, New York City, N.Y., 1998, p. 353.

9. *St. Paul Recorder*, 24 February 1972.

10. *St. Paul Recorder*, 16 March 1972.

11. *St. Paul Recorder*, 5 April 1972.

12. *St. Paul Recorder*, 4 May 1972.

13. Williams, Juan, *Thurgood Marshall: American Revolutionary*, p. 359.

14. *St. Paul Recorder*, 10 August 1972.

15. *St. Paul Recorder*, 16 November 1972.

16. *St. Paul Recorder*, 27 November 1972.

17. *St. Paul Recorder*, 14 December 1972.

18. *St. Paul Recorder*, 15 March 1973.

19. *St. Paul Recorder*, 11 October 1973.

20. *St. Paul Recorder*, 13 December 1973.

21. *St. Paul Recorder*, 4 April 1974.

22. *St. Paul Recorder*, 13 December 1974.

23. *St. Paul Recorder*, 20 December 1974.

24. *St. Paul Recorder*, 27 March 1975.

25. *St. Paul Recorder*, 29 May 1975.

26. *St. Paul Recorder*, 30 October 1974. (In the U.S. Supreme Court's first major race relations decision in 1980, Thurgood Marshall was successful in Fullilove v. Klutznick, in convincing his colleagues to vote 6–3, in the affirmative and allow Congress to grant employers the right to contract set-aside programs for minority businesses and their employees.)

27. *St. Paul Recorder*, 27 November 1975.

28. *St. Paul Recorder*, 8 January 1976.

29. *St. Paul Recorder*, 29 January 1976.

30. Griffin, James, with Kwame McDonald, *Jimmy Griffin, Son of Rondo: A Memoir,* Ramsey County Historical Society, St. Paul, Minnesota, 2001, pp. 93–94.

31. *St. Paul Recorder*, 22 September 1977.

32. Jimmy Griffin: *A Son of Rondo, A Memoir.* p. 121.

33. *St. Paul Recorder*, 13 October 1977.

34. *St. Paul Recorder*, 15 December 1977.

35. William, Juan, *Thurgood Marshall: American Revolutionary*, p. 367.

36. *St. Paul Recorder*, 16 November 1978.

37. *St. Paul Recorder*, 13 September 1979.

38. *St. Paul Recorder*, 1 November 1979.

39. *St. Paul Recorder*, 29 November 1979.

40. ibid..

41. Poinsett, Alex, *Walking with Presidents, Louis Martin and the Rise of Black Political Power*, Rowan and Littlefield Publisher Inc., New York, 1997, p. 186.

42. Bass, Jack,, T*aming the Storm: The Life and Times of Judge Frank M. Johnson Jr., and the South's Fight Over Civil Rights,* Anchor Book, Doubleday, New York, 1993, p. 367.

EPILOGUE
1980 - 1985

"It must be borne in mind that the tragedy in life doesn't lie in not reaching your goal. The tragedy lies in having no goal to reach. It isn't a calamity to die with dreams unfulfilled, but it is a calamity not to dream. It is not a disaster to be unable to capture your ideal, but it is a disaster to have no ideal to capture. It is not a disgrace not to reach the stars, but it is a disgrace to have no stars to reach for. Not failure, but low aim is a sin."

Inscription on the tombstone of Benjamin E. Mays (1895-1984)

Early in 1980, Georgia Senator Julian Bond came to St. Paul on behalf of African-American city council candidate Bill Wilson. He spoke at some of the precinct caucuses and to those who had been elected as delegates to the city convention.

At the convention, Richard Radman, who was president of the St. Paul Building Trades Association, nominated Wilson and State Representative Fred Norton, who was Speaker of the House, seconded his nomination. Despite these strong endorsements, Wilson received slightly less than 20 percent of the 60 percent needed and was forced into a run-off with fellow candidates Carol Connolly and Todd Lefko. In March, Wilson won the primary race against Lefko by a vote of 6,280 to 5,445.[1]

Bill Wilson

Despite his clear victory, Fourth District Associate Chairperson, Jan Dietrich, petitioned the Fourth District Central Committee to call a special session of its 72 delegates who then voted to endorse Lefko for

213

Council Seat F. This was done despite the fact that the 580 city convention delegates voted not to endorse any candidate for Council Seat F, for which Wilson and Lefko were contending. Their actions also ignored the fact that since the beginning of the DFL party, in 1948, the endorsement for office had always gone to the winner of the primary. Wilson did not indulge in name-calling or finger-pointing, but took the position that, "Clearly, the endorsement by the DFL was wrong, but we'll let the people of St. Paul decide." In April, Wilson was elected by a vote of 19,600 to Lefko's 17,066.[2]

In Washington, the first major race relations case of the 1980s was being argued in Fullilove v. Klutznick, which dealt with the constitutionality of set-aside contracts similar to those the St. Paul Urban League had benefited from during the previous decade. With the help of Justice Marshall's constant arguments in conferences, the Court voted 6–3 in favor of the government setting aside ten percent of its contracts for minority businesses and workers. His argument that such programs did disadvantage some whites, but not whites as a class won over the Court's majority.

In June, Coretta Scott King congratulated St. Paul's US Representative Bruce Vento for his co-authorship of a bill which established the Martin Luther King Jr. National Historic District site in Atlanta and told reporters that, "The work and commitment on his part not only assured the preservation of the Sweet Auburn Landmark District, but also the revitalization of our entire community."

In July, Arthur McWatt was appointed Chairman of the St. Paul Human Rights Commission and was immediately caught up in what Alvin Poussaint had warned minority communities of color, of the increasing attempts by feminist groups to wrest control of human rights organizations. There was such a group on the St. Paul Commission. The rancorous debate and lack of civility reached its peak when one commissioner walked out in the middle of an Executive Director job interview of an out-state male minority candidate with the excuse that she had a "more important appointment." The turmoil finally ended with the election of a compromise candidate, who happened to be the current Assistant Executive Director, whom neither faction felt comfortable with and after it was discovered that the current staff did not reflect the gender nor cultural diversity of St. Paul, McWatt decided to tender his resignation.

At the end of the year, City Councilman Bill Wilson introduced a resolution making January 15th Martin Luther King Day in St. Paul, which was unanimously adopted by the City Council.[3]

The following January, a new era of wealth and privilege began in America with the 16 million dollar inauguration of Ronald Reagan, which author Haynes Johnson called a "Bacchanalia of the Haves."[4] The new President had a long held philosophy that, "Government was not the solution to our problems; but was the problem." It became one of the dominant themes of his administration during the first term. Its result served to unleash much of the inherent destructiveness of an unregulated market economy, which escalated the national debt to the point that made social reform difficult if not impossible. It also reversed most of the civil rights gains which had been made over the past three decades.

The new administration was not only indifferent to social reform, they were hostile to it. Reagan's style of governing was nondirective and his popularity was helped by his movie persona and his skills as a communicator and entertainer. He was often compared to his favorite President, Calvin Coolidge, who served during the time Reagan was in college. Coolidge and Reagan both appeared to have been men who had, "second class minds but first class temperaments." An emerging New Right made up of evangelical fundamentalists, wealthy, laissez-faire conservatives, anti-union businessmen and the politically oft-ignored western and southern Republicans, bolstered Reagan's constituency.

Reagan had been immensely impressed by the wealthy since his second marriage and began to enjoy the role of protector of the status quo of the rich. One way he discovered to protect their wealth was to hold down inflation by increasing unemployment. His Budget Director, David Stockman, encouraged him in this direction and even noted in an address to the U.S. Chamber of Commerce that, "unemployment is part of our cure for inflation." This was echoed by Press Secretary Larry Speakes' statement to reporters a short time later that, "unemployment is the price that must be paid to bring down inflation."[5]

His policy of unemployment was most harmful to the poor and particularly African-Americans who since 1940 have had almost twice the unemployment figures of whites annually. It hastened the development of what came to be known as the underclass.

Reaganomics also dramatically increased the importation of cheap foreign goods as well as an increase in immigration which hastened the deindustrialization of the economy and served to downsize the nation's work force into lower-paying service jobs.

By the end of Reagan's first term, Dr. Robert Hill, the Urban League's Director of Research in his annual "State of Black America Report" warned that, "there are alarming numbers of African-American men who simply can no longer earn enough to support a wife and child."[6] This has resulted in a dramatic increase in single mothers and welfare recipients in African-American communities.

From the beginning, Reagan individualized the systemic problem of race by simply eliminating the term from all his public utterances.[7]

His "New Beginnings" theme for schools was based on the Miliken v. Bradley Decision of 1974, which ruled against any inter-district school desegregation between urban and suburban school districts. He helped to defeat the Equal Rights Amendment for women and weakened affirmative action by undermining the Office of Federal Contract Compliance and reducing its number of compliance officers by 60 percent as well as its compliance agreements by over 70 percent.[8] He reversed an eleven-year policy of denying tax-exempt status to private schools and colleges who practiced racial discrimination, and fought eleven months against the extension of the Voting Rights Law. By the end of his first term, Reagan had further weakened the protection of civil rights by appointing judges who were ideologically opposed to the entire body of case law in the area of racial discrimination and an Assistant Attorney General for Civil Rights, W. Bradford Reynolds, who was actively working to abrogate Executive Order 11246.[9]

In St. Paul, during Reagan's first term, agitators, advocates and activists were desperately trying to hold on to what years of struggle had won. Agencies and civil rights groups that had been dependent upon governmental and local funding became more conservative. Activists and advocates such as Clarence Mitchell and Roy Wilkins died while others like Vernon Jordan had become endangered species whose lives had been threatened.

Three of the bright stars who were able to sustain their positions of militant protest in the St. Paul's African-American community during those years were Mahmoud El-Kati, a brilliant Macalester College teacher, who maintained his social utilitarian role of intellectualizing and interpreting the African-American struggle for a myriad of social and class levels in the community and in the process sacrificed to a significant degree any opportunity he had to pursue higher academic honors, tenure and prestige.

Mahmoud El-Kati

During his continuing tenure he worked with Twin City Urban Leagues, Sabathani Community Center and The Way. He conducted a weekly Marketplace Community Seminar in both cities, served on the boards of North Central Voters League and the Youth Services Bureau, and lectured at many institutions of higher learning as well as giving talks at countless secondary and elementary schools. He also served on the staffs of many educational institutes, resource and study centers and conducted workshops on African-American history.

Nathaniel A. Khaliq

The second activist was Nathaniel Abdul Khaliq (Nick Davis), who worked as a firefighter, a housing project owner/manager and St. Paul NAACP President. Khaliq had demonstrated courage in his numerous confrontations with racist and criminal elements in St. Paul such as his successful campaigns to close down a local theatre showing pornographic films and to eliminate prostitution on the community's main northern perimeter. Khaliq was politically involved and ran in a city council primary race. As President of the St. Paul NAACP, he was continually militant and articulate in the civil rights struggle in the streets and in St. Paul's various institutions.

The third star in the galaxy of heroes is the Reverend James W. Battle, who received his early civil rights baptism in Ypsilanti, Michigan, during the 1960s, where he led a boycott against his employers at Ford Motor Company and in the process politically mobilized the local population to elect their first African-American mayor. After completing his ministerial training at the American Baptist Institute, Battle helped organize the St. Paul Ministerial Alliance in the 1970s and initiated the celebration of Dr. Martin Luther King Jr. Day in African-American churches and helped organize the first Martin Luther King March in 1979, which had 5,000 participants. In the 1980s, he was co-chair with State Senator Randy Staten of a committee, which placed a bust of Dr. Martin Luther King Jr. in the State Capitol rotunda.

All three careers were of inestimable value in sustaining community morale and hope during the Reagan onslaught. Unfortunately, during this period many urban agencies became mere caretakers or custodians of a former legacy of vigilant and aggressive public trust. Their heads often managed to keep themselves busy by serving on a multiplicity of corporate and institutional boards. Also, many minority members of their former boards followed their middle-class white neighbors to the suburbs which left a vacuum of leadership.

My purpose in compiling this chronicle has been an attempt to show that our city has been blessed with a rich heritage of strong and imaginative leadership over the past century. It has also been an effort to show that St. Paul has often been the training ground for civil rights leaders throughout the nation, many of whom learned their crafts here.

The names of Frederick L. McGhee, W.T. Francis, Nellie Griswald Francis, Father Stephen Theobald, Monsignor Francis Gilligan, the Reverend T.R. Nelson, the Reverend Floyd Massey, Clarence Carter, Roy Wilkins, Clarence Mitchell, Allie Mae Hampton, S. Vincent Owens, Estyr B. Peake, Louis Ervin, Lawrence Borom, Katie McWatt, Leonard Carter, the Reverend James Battle, Nathaniel Abdul Khaliq and Vice-Presidents Hubert Humphrey and Walter Mondale were all nurtured on the protest tradition that had been carried on by the crusading journalism of J.Q. Adams, Earl Wilkins, and Cecil Newman. This legacy, which author William Banks lauds bore fruit for St. Paulites, for over a century and provided them both strength and support to carry on their struggle.[10] What these persons had in common was an appreciation and a dedication to the First, Fifth and Fourteenth Amendments to the Constitution and the desire to make the public aware, through their ability to articulate needs and the courage to confront bigotry and institutional racism wherever they found it. They were of many races and creeds and colors and of both genders and they all served to improve the lives of not just their constituents, but the lives of all those in their communities, their city, their state and their nation.

EPILOGUE BIBLIOGRAPHY

1. *St. Paul Recorder*, 20 March 1980.

2. *St. Paul Recorder*, 10 April 1980.

3. *St. Paul Recorder*, 4 December 1980.

4. Johnson, Haynes, *Sleepwalking Through History*, W.W. Norton Publisher, New York, 1991, p. 20

5. ibid.. p. 82.

6. Franklin, John Hope, *The Color Line: Legacy for the Twenty-First Century*, University of Missouri Press, Columbia, Missouri, 1990, p. 19.

7. ibid.. p. 370.

8. Meyers, Samuel L. Jr., *Civil Rights and Race Relations in the Post Reagan-Bush Era,* Praeger Press, Westport, Connecticut, p. 57.

9. ibid.. p. 220.

10. Banks, William M. *Black Intellectuals: Race and Responsibility in American Life*, W.W. Norton Publishers, New York City, NY, 1996, p. 15.

Biography of Arthur McWatt

Arthur Chandler McWatt was born in St. Paul, Minnesota and still resides in the city. McWatt received his early education at Drew Elementary and Mechanic Arts High School. He earned a Bachelors Degree in Education and a Masters Degree in History at the University of Minnesota. While at the U of M, McWatt became a member of Alpha Phi Alpha fraternity. He was selected for the Experienced Teachers Fellowship, which allowed him to conduct graduate studies at the East West Center of the University of Hawaii.

Arthur McWatt

An early interest in seeing an end to discrimination led McWatt to serve in vital roles on the Catholic Inter-Racial Committee, the St. Paul Human Rights Commission and the St. Paul NAACP.

McWatt was a member of the Ramsey County Preservation Committee and served with Virginia Kunz on the Ramsey County History Editorial Board. He has written about African American's history and culture in St. Paul and has published articles in various periodicals.

Small and Cohesive: St. Paul's Resourceful African-American Community,
   Ramsey County History (1991)

Growing up in St. Paul Down St. Alban's Hill in a Wooden Coaster Wagon,
   Ramsey County History, (1996).

A Greater Victory: The Brotherhood of Sleeping Car Porters in St. Paul,
   Minnesota History (1997).

McWatt retired from 33 years of teaching history in the St. Paul Public Schools with particular focus on African American, Native American, Mexican American, Russian and Asian experiences. His book *Crusaders for Justice* is the result of several years of study and research about the culture and history of St. Paul's African American population. His book seeks to spotlight some of those advocates, activists and agitators who were in the vanguard of the civil and human rights movement locally and nationally.

Arthur and his wife Katie are the parents of Tim, Stacy, Chris and Lynn. They are grandparents of Danae, Austin, Cole, Reid, Croix and Cade.

Photos of Arthur & Katie McWatt

INDEX

Adams, Eloise 179

Adams, John (J.Q.) .21-22, 24-25, 27, 37, 39-45,
53-54, 56-57, 59, 62, 92, 201, 219

Adkins, Alpha 142, 170, 181, 189

Adkins, Lonnie 176, 191

Anderson, Governor C. Elmer 134, 137, 138, 153, 162-163, 165, 167

Anderson, Evan 57, 181

Anderson, Marian 91, 141

Anderson, Olga 118

Anderson, Governor Wendell 190

Affirmative Action 163, 174, 182-183, 192, 204, 206-207, 216

Afro-American Enforcement League 23, 27, 31

Anti-Lynching Bills 55-57, 66, 86, 88, 199

Battle, Reverend W. James 218

Benner, Bradford 177

Black Migration 6, 46-47

Borom, Lawrence 181-182, 189, 194, 197, 219

Boyd, Frank 60, 82, 86, 103, 109, 131

Carter, Elmer 59, 63, 138

Carter, President Jimmy 202, 208

Carter, Leonard 148, 150, 152-154, 160, 173

Carty, Rev. Denzil 148, 150, 160-164, 167-168,
170, 176, 179-180, 182, 190, 193

225

Catholic Interracial Councils 84, 151, 154-155, 167-168, 173

Census 1859 (MN) 6

Census 1860 (MN) 10

Census 1890 (MN) 21

Census 1865 (St.Paul) 15

Census 1868 (St. Paul) 16

Census 1910 (US) 41

Census 1915-1920 (St. Paul/MN) 46-47

Census 1930 (St. Paul) 73-74

Census of 1940 (St. Paul) 101

Census or 1950 (US) 127

Census on Voting in the South 1965–1968 .180

Census on Blacks in Elective Office 1970 187

Civil Rights, Origin of 21

Civil Rights Law of 1875 17

Civil Rights Law of 1885 27

Civil Rights Law of 1957 148

Cooper, Ernest 138, 148, 153

Culver, John 92

Donnelly, Ignatius . . . . .xi, 9, 11

Douglass, Frederick 16, 17, 21, 53, 166

DuBois, W.E.B. 33-34, 36, 46, 80, 85, 127, 168, 179

Duluth Lynching 54-56, 61

El-Kati, Mahmoud 182, 217

INDEX

Equal Rights League 46, 60, 61

Ervin, Louis, J Attorney 39, 42, 55,74-75, 87-88

Ervin, Louis 101, 148, 177

FEPC 104, 111-112, 119, 128, 130-131
134, 136, 141-142, 147, 151, 163-165

Fox, Richard 141-142, 164

Francis, Nellie Griswold 55-56, 66, 114

Francis, William Trevanne 36-38, 41-43, 53, 57-58, 60-61, 66, 78

Freeman, Governor Orville 142, 150-151, 153, 159, 164

Galloway, Flora 168

Galloway, Jon 200

Gilligan, Rev. Francis J. 85-86, 117-118, 135-138, 149, 155, 163

Green, Maymie 148

Griffin, J.M 24-26

Griffin, James S 193-194, 203

Hall, S. Edward 58-59, 92, 109

Hall, O.C 37-39, 45

Hampton, Allie Mae 134, 142, 164-165

Harris, Rev. Lee W. 86

Harris, Reginald 99, 181-182

Harris, Robert 195, 199

Hilyard, Gale 56

Holland, George 91, 100, 136, 192

Housing Laws and Regulations 47, 118, 134, 137, 144, 146, 149-150
152-153, 163, 169-170, 172, 176, 178-179, 183, 192

227

Howard, Timothy 150, 153

Howell, Owen 58, 61-62, 74

Human Rights Ordinance in St. Paul 146, 172, 199

Humphrey, Senator Hubert 113, 120, 130, 139, 161, 171-172
174, 180, 193, 196, 202, 204, 219

Ireland, Archbishop John 15-16, 22-24, 40

Jacobowski, Daniel 163

James, Charles 27, 33

Johnson, Josie 163, 176, 190

Khaliq, Abdul Nathaniel 218

Lang, Toni 174

Latimer, Mayor George 202, 205

Lewis, Donald 172, 182, 190, 199

LeVander, Governor Harold 176-177, 188

Littlejohn, Maceo 99, 107, 197

Lyles, T.H 21, 78

Lyles, T.H. Mrs 32, 37, 40

Marshall, Governor William R. 10, 13-14, 16

Massey, Floyd Jr 135, 137, 148

Maxwell, Ethel Howard 42, 152

Maxwell, Stephen 117, 148, 151-152

McDonald, James (Kwame) 164-165, 167, 170

McGhee, Frederick L 23, 27, 31-36, 189

McWatt, Katie 169-170, 176, 179, 180-182, 189, 197, 202, 204-205

INDEX

Minnesota Federation of Colored Women 32, 42

Minnesota Colored Home Guard 45

Minnesota Negro Labor Council 86

Mitchell, Clarence 89-91, 105-106, 121, 144, 160, 171, 176, 183

Mondale, Senator Walter 172, 174, 178, 198, 199, 201, 202

Morris, William 27

Nelson, Reverend T.R. 116, 135

Newman, Cecil 71-73, 75-76, 78-79, 81-89, 91-93, 100, 104, 110-113
        116, 121, 128, 132-134, 145, 154, 161 166-167, 171, 179, 188, 201

North Central Voters League 170, 176, 217

Owens, Vincent S 104-107, 111, 115, 120, 129-130, 134

Peake, Estyr Bradley 189

Pillow, Edgar 195, 199

Ransom, Samuel 44, 104, 110, 117

Reed, Samuel 102, 106, 115

Robbins, Jerry 150

Rogers, Charles 105, 109, 116, 118

Rucker, Clifford 86, 88-89, 118, 129, 131, 136, 148, 163

St. Paul Council of Human Relations 113, 115, 117, 132-133, 162

St. Paul Urban Coalition 179, 189, 191, 194, 207

Scheiner, Samuel 100, 174

Schwartz, Jonas G 100, 175

Scrutchin, Charles W 27, 55

Shannon, George 60

229

Smalls, Robert 65-66, 73

Smith, O Donald 168, 198

Smith, Frank 146, 148, 179

Smith, Lena O 56, 76

Smith, Nathaniel J 129, 160

Sternberg, Arthur 116

Talley, Thomas 137-138

Theobald, Stephen Reverend 35, 39-40, 76-78, 135

Thye, Governor Edward J. 136, 167

Turner, Valdo 35-37, 40, 53-54, 58-61, 75

Twin City Protective League 35-36

St. Paul Colored Voters League 60

Wheaton, J. Francis 26-27, 57

Wilkins, Earl 47, 61-65

Wilkins, Roy 58-60, 76, 79-80, 82, 142-143, 160, 201

Wilson, William "Bill" 208, 213-215

Windom, Senator William 14

Young, Whitney 118, 122, 187, 190

Youngdahl, Governor Luther 113, 117, 130-131, 151, 155

BOOK BIBLIOGRAPHY

Chapter One:

Flandrau, Charles E. *History of Minnesota*, E.W. Porter Publisher, 1900.

Spangler, Earl, *The Negro in Minnesota*, Y.S. Denison and Company Publisher, Minneapolis, MN., 1961.

Chapter Two:

Carly, Kenneth, *Minnesota in the Civil War*, Ross and Haines Incorporated Publishers, Minneapolis, MN. 1961.

Glatthaar, Joseph T., *Forged in Battle; The Civil War Alliance of Black Soldiers and White Officers*, The Free Press, New York City, NY, 1990.

McFeely, William *S. Frederick Douglass*, W.W. Norton and Company, New York City, NY, 1991

Moynihan, James H., *The Life and Archbishop John Ireland*, Harper and Brothers Publisher, New York City, NY, 1953.

Nelson, Paul D., Frederick L. McGhee; *A Life on the Color Line 1861-1912*, Minnesota Historical Society Press, St. Paul, MN, 2002.

O'Connell, Marvin R. O., *John Ireland and the American Catholic Church*, Minnesota Historical Society, St. Paul, MN, 1988.

Chapter Three:

Spangler, Earl, *The Negro in Minnesota*, T.S. Denison and Company, Minneapolis, MN, 1961.

Nelson, Paul D., *Frederick L. McGhee; A Life on the Color Line: 1861-1912*, Minnesota Historical Society, St. Paul, Minnesota, 2002.

Chapter Four:

Baker, Ray Strannard, *Following the Color Line*, Harpers Row, New York City, NY, 1964.

Chapter Five:

Fedo, Michael W., *They was Just Niggers; An Account of One of the Nation's Least Know Tragedies*, Brasch and Brasch Publisher, Inc., Ontario, California, 1979.

Griffin, James, *Blacks in the St. Paul Fire Department; 1885-1976*, E. And J. Publishers, St. Paul, MN. 1976.

Madigan, Tim, *The Burning: Massacre, Destruction and the Tulsa Riot of 1921*, Thomas Dunne Books, St. Martin Press, New York, 2001.

Chapter Six:

Leopold, L.E. *Cecil E. Newman: Newspaper Publisher*, T.S. Denison & Company, Minneapolis, MN, 1969.

Chapter Seven:

Anderson, Jervis, *A. Philip Randolph; A Biographical Portrait*, Harcort Brace, New York, 1972.

Aston, Gerald, *The Right to Fight*, Presido Press Vocato, California, 1998.

Dickerson, Dennis C. *Militant Mediator; Whitney M. Young Jr.*, The University of Kentucky Press, Lexington, Kentucky, 1998.

Frances, Charles, R., *The Tuskegee Airmen; The Men Who Changed the Nation*, Brandon Publishing Company, Boston, MA, 1988.

Haywood, Wil, *King of the Cats; The Life Times of Adam Clayton Powell*, Houghton and Mifflin Company, New York, 1993.

Rose Robert A. D.D.S., *Lonely Eagles: The Story of America's Black Air Force in World War II*, Tuskegee Airmen Inc., 1976.

Williams, Juan, *Thurgood Marshall; American Revolutionary* Random House, New York City, NY, 1996.

BIBLIOGRAPHY

Chapter Eight:

Bass, Jack, *Taming of the Storm; The Life and Times of Judge Frank M. Johnson Jr., and the South's Fight Over Civil Rights,* Anchor Books, Doubleday, New York, 1993.

Duberman, Martin, *Paul Robeson: A Biography*, The New Press, New York, 1989.

Watson, Denton L. *Lion in the Lobby; Clarence Mitchell Jr.'s Struggle for the Passage of Civil Rights Laws*, William Morrow and Company Inc., New York, 1990.

Chapter Nine:

Grant, Joanne, *Ella Baker; Freedom Bound*, John Wiley & Sons, New York, 1998.

Humphrey, Hubert H., *The Education of a Public Man; My Life and Politics*, University of Minnesota Press, Minneapolis, MN., 1991.

Lewis, John, *Walking with the Wind; A Memoir of the Movement*, Simon and Schuster, New York City, NY, 1998.

Poinsett, Alex, *Walking with Presidents; Louis Martin and the Rise of Black Political Power,* Rowmand and Littlefield Publisher, New York, 1997.

Young, Andrew, *An Easy Burden; The Civil Rights Movement and the Transformation of America*, Harper Publishers, New York City, NY, 1996.

Chapter Ten:

James Griffin with Kwame McDonald, *Jimmy Griffin, Son of Rondo; A Memoir*, Ramsey County Historical Society, St. Paul, MN, 2001.

Williams, Juan, *Thurgood Marshall; American Revolutionary*, Random House, New York City, NY, 1996.

Epilogue:

Banks, William M. *Black Intellectuals; Race and Responsibility in American Life*, W.W. Norton Publishers, New York City, NY, 1996.

Franklin, John Hope, *The Color Line; Legacy for the Twenty-First Century*, University of Missouri Press, Columbia, Missouri, 1990.

Johnson, Haynes, *Sleepwalking through History*, W.W. Norton Publisher, New York City, NY, 1991.

Meyers, Samuel L. Jr., *Civil Rights and Race Relations in the Post Reagan-Bush Era*, Praeger Press, Wesport, Connecticut.

Reference Books

Low, Augustus and Clift, *Virgil A., Encyclopedia of Black America*, McGraw Hill Book Company, New York City, NY, 1981.

Berman, Peter, M., *The Chronological History of the Negro in America*, Harper and Row Publishers, New York City, NY, 1969.

Photo Credits

Chapter 1

George Bonga, Charles Alfred Zimmerman - MNHS 2

Chapter 2

Robert Hickman, Minnesota Historical Society 11

Chapter 3

John Ireland, Minnesota Historical Society 23
J. Q. Adams, Minnesota Historical Society 25
J. F. Wheaton, Charles Alfred Zimmerman - MNHS 26

Chapter 4

Mrs. T. H. Lyles, Kregel Photo Parlors- MNHS 32
W.E.B. Dubois, Papyrus Publishing Inc. 34
Frederick McGhee, Minnesota Historical Society 35
Father Stephen Theobald, Minnesota Historical Society .39
Ethel Howard Maxwell, Stephen Maxwell 42

Chapter 6

Cecil Newman, Rohn Engh - MNHS 72
Frank Boyd, Buzz Brown Photographic Studios - MNHS 86

Chapter 7

Whitney Young, Minnesota Historical Society 118

Chapter 8

Thurgood Marshall, Cecil Layne - MNHS 140
Roy Wilkins, Cecil Layne - MNHS 143
Reverend Denzil Carty, Papyrus Publishing Inc. 150

Chapter 9

Martin Luther King Jr., Cecil Layne - MNHS 163
Katie McWatt, A & K McWatt. 170
Odessa Bond, A & K McWatt 182

Chapter 10

Estyr Bradley Peake, Minnesota Historical Society 190

Josie Johnson, Josie Johnson 190

Epilogue

Bill Wilson, Charles Chamblis - MNHS 213
Mahmoud El-Kati, Mahmoud El-Kati 217
Abdul Khaliq, Abdul Khaliq 218

Biography

Arthur McWatt #1,A & K McWatt 221
Arthur McWatt Military Photo #1, A & K McWatt 222
Arthur McWatt Military Photo #2, A & K McWatt 222
Arthur McWatt& Friends Military Photo, A & K McWatt 222
Arthur McWatt 1950s, A & K McWatt 222
Katie McWatt #1, A & K McWatt 223
Katie McWatt #2, A & K McWatt 223
Katie McWatt #3, A & K McWatt 223
Katie McWatt #4, A & K McWatt 223
Arthur McWatt w/Obama button, A & K McWatt 223
Arthur McWatt w/Lake background, A & K McWatt 223
Arthur and Katie McWatt, A & K McWatt 223

Cover
Composite photo mosaic made from the photographs in this book